Food

FOR BEGINNERS

Susan George & Nigel Paige

Writers and Readers

Writers and Readers Publishing Cooperative Society Ltd.
144 Camden High Street, London NW1 0NE, England

Published by Writers and Readers Publishing
Cooperative Society Ltd. 1982

Series Editor Richard Appignanesi
Text Copyright © 1982 Susan George
Illustrations Copyright © 1982 Nigel Paige
Cover design by Louise Fili

Printed in Great Britain at
The University Press, Oxford

Cased: ISBN 0 906495 85 7
Paper: ISBN 0 906495 84 9

Food Is Power

Hungry?

Hungry? If you were born in the right part of the world and into the right social class, the solution to your problem is no farther away than the nearest refrigerator.

If you weren't, then you may go hungry all your short life, as 800 million people do, who were born in the wrong place and into the wrong social class.

Lots of people, frankly, are tired of hearing about them and their problems, which seem eternal and inevitable.

NOT SO.

The reasons people go hungry are not mysterious. Mass starvation is not an act of God. Hunger is created and maintained by human decisions, by minorities who benefit from under-development. What has been done by some can be undone by others, if they learn to use their own strength.

Our distant ancestors got their food through hunting and gathering. This is an excellent system if the climate is warm enough and if there are only a few people per square mile. Hunter-gatherers have, at their own very low level of material wants, quite a good life. They have almost no possessions (which are heavy and hamper mobility), but on their own terms, they enjoy exceptional abundance and leisure. "Primitive" people share with each other and would be shocked at the mere suggestion that food is a commodity to be bought and sold. Food means life and mother. Would you sell your mother?

One hunter-gatherer can feed four or five people,* which means that a !Kung bushman is as efficient as an American farmer in 1870 or a French one in 1938, though he needs much more space.

* The ! signals a click in the !Kung San language. The rest of us do not get exclamation marks.

1 Hunter Gatherers (HGs FOR SHORT)

7

If HGs enjoyed the "original affluent society", why did people ever bother to start farming as they did between 12,000 and 5,000 years ago? The archeological evidence suggests different reasons for different parts of the world. In some places, the climate became less favourable, obliging people to store food during the cold or dry seasons.

Or the numbers of humans and animals increased, causing greater competition for food. Some aspect of HGs' lives deteriorated. Otherwise they would have kept on practicing a good thing.

8

2 Agriculture

The beginnings of agriculture have been called the Neolithic (Stone Age) Revolution, but this term is misleading because farming did not replace hunting and gathering overnight. Sometimes they coexisted for centuries or millenia, and any one group might do both simultaneously (like many American Indians). This "revolution" was more like getting drunk or falling in love: easy to recognise after the fact, but not always apparent at the time.

9

In most places, ever since people started
farming for a living, HGs haven't had a
moment's peace. They have had to compete
with farmers for land they once roamed freely,
and the farmers have invariably won.

In every area where scholars can trace the
moving frontier between farmers and HGs,
there is archeological evidence of fighting. This
process of elimination of HGs has continued
during our own lifetimes.

So, agriculture is a very recent phenomenon in
human history:

Approx. 10,000 years farming = **0.0025% of Human existence**
4,000.000 years since 1st humans

But as far as we're concerned, it's the 0.0025%
that counts. No one, outside of the odd freak or
saintly hermit, would want to go back to the
Stone Age even, if we could.

3 What's Good About Farming?

Here are some of the things the farming revolution has made possible:

1. **We can live in larger, stable communities.** HGs have to live in very small, mobile groups — but most humans are gregarious and prefer villages, towns or cities.

2. **We can do different kinds of work.** HGs **all** have to concentrate on the food supply; but with agriculture, specialisation becomes possible. If you don't care for raising crops and animals, you can learn to make rush roofs and baskets or clay pots or leather goods. Farming spells the beginnings of the "division of labour".

3. **We can have some belongings of our own.**
HGs possess almost nothing, but with settlement, material goods can be accumulated, and more or less permanent dwellings built. **Food** itself is the first material good to be accumulated. Our impulse for permanence may be satisfied with anything from decorated cooking pots and thatched huts to video cassettes and imitation Tudor suburban houses. But most of us enjoy owning some possessions and appreciate good food, clothing and shelter.

4. **We can think about something besides our daily bread** (or our daily nuts, berries and gazelle steak). Without farming and the stable communities it allows, you wouldn't have much in the way of art, music, architecture, philosophy, or Beginners Books. (OK, OK, so there are Neolithic paintings at Lascaux and in the Hoggar, but you see what we mean.) Culture and farming go together. Both imply stability, permanence and a belief in the future.

We haven't obtained the benefits of agriculture without paying for them, and some have paid more dearly than others. It seems a general rule that, as soon as our species settles down, some of its members will try to obtain their food supply without working, by controlling the land and the people who cultivate it. Those in positions of power are thus guaranteed their dinners, even in lean years. Farming also means the beginning of unequal distribution of wealth (land and food **are** wealth) and the division of society into dominated and dominating classes. The latter, understandably from their point of view, soon find it expedient to establish police forces and bureaucracies to help keep food producers "in their place". There are no historical instances where the peasants have been their own rulers for more than very short periods.

The whole point of growing crops is to be able to store them — this is how one gains some hold upon the future. The granary is the embryo of the State. In ancient Morocco, the same word — "makhzen" — meant both "granary" and "government".

States develop military hardware to protect their food supply from outsiders and to extend their control as far as possible into the hinterland — thus ensuring even larger food supplies under their control. No farms without arms.

16

There are rare cases where everyone who wants a piece of land to farm can have one, and where cooperative farming is undertaken by the community. This kind of agriculture — once more common — still exists in parts of Africa and among some tribal people in India.

But usually, a small group of individuals with close ties and common interests hog the land for themselves and leave little or none to the great mass of the people who have to work as slaves, serfs, share-croppers, tenants, casual labourers or what-have-you. They may work for a king, a religious body, a chieftain, a feudal lord, a gentleman or a richer peasant. Historically, there has been a huge variety of land-tenure arrangements and of employers and there still is today. So there are a hundred and one different ways of being poor.

17

Concentration of power over food and food producing resources in just a few hands, whatever its nature, always has been and still is the main cause of hunger.

Today, slaves and serfs are obsolete in most societies. On the other hand, there are millions of supposedly "free" farmers working small plots of land. The luckiest can feed themselves and their families year-around on what they produce (this is called "self-provisioning".) Many cannot, and must supplement their income through outside work, or borrowing.

4 Peasants

Stragely enough, it is these very people who live in the countryside, and produce the food, who are the first to go hungry — the peasantry. Here is a good definition of the peasantry:

" The peasantry consists of small agricultural producers who, with the help of simple equipment and the labour of their families, produce mainly for their own consumption and for the fulfilment of obligations to the holders of political and economic power."

"Holders of political and economic power", depending on just how powerful they are, use a variety of more or less extortionate measures for extracting wealth from people in the countryside.

YOU CAN CONDUCT YOUR OWN EXAMINATION OF HOW THIS IS DONE IN A GIVEN PAST OR PRESENT-DAY SOCIETY BY FILLING IN A TABLE LIKE THIS ONE:

OBLIGATIONS TO THE HOLDERS OF POLITICAL AND ECONOMIC POWER

	CASH	KIND INCLUDING WORK
FIXED		
PROPORTIONAL (TO PRODUCTION OR INCOME)		

A HEAD-TAX OR A SET RENT WOULD PUT AN X IN THE FIXED/CASH SLOT. A TITHE OF PRODUCE TO THE CHURCH, OR THE VARYING NUMBER OF BUSHELS OF WHEAT OWED A LANDLORD BY A SHARECROPPER WOULD BELONG TO PROPORTIONAL/KIND. A NUMBER OF COMPULSORY WORK-DAYS PER WEEK OR YEAR ON SOMEONE ELSE'S LAND IS FIXED/KIND. OUR OWN INCOME TAXES ARE PROPORTIONAL/CASH. AND SO ON.

PROPORTIONAL OBLIGATION

SAY A PEASANT OWES 40% OF HIS HARVEST: IF A GOOD YEAR'S HARVEST IS 100 UNITS, THE LANDLORD GETS 40 AND THE PEASANT KEEPS 60 FOR HIS NEEDS.

IF A BAD YEAR'S HARVEST DROPS TO 80 UNITS THE LANDLORD'S SHARE OF 40% IS THEN 32 AND THE PEASANT'S FALLS BY 1/5 TO 48.

HOW DOES ALL THIS LOOK TO THE PEASANT? GRIM!
BUT IT'S MUCH GRIMMER FOR HIM WHEN HIS
OBLIGATIONS ARE FIXED. AGRICULTURE IS BY NATURE
·····REALLY BY NATURE····· AN UP AND DOWN
ACTIVITY. THERE ARE GOOD HARVESTS AND BAD ONES
AND IN A BAD YEAR A FIXED RENT TAKES A WORSE
CHUNK OUT OF THE PEASANT'S LIVELIHOOD THAN
WOULD A PROPORTION OF THE HARVEST.
AN EXAMPLE OF THE TWO SYSTEMS ARE BELOW.

FIXED OBLIGATION

A GOOD YEAR'S PRODUCE IS 100 UNITS THE LANDLORD GETS A FIXED 40 AND THE PEASANT STILL KEEPS 60.

BUT IF A BAD YEARS HARVEST IS 80 UNITS THE LANDLORD STILL GETS HIS FIXED 40, WHILE THE PEASANTS SHARE FALLS BY 1/3 TO 40. 8 LESS THAN WITH PROPORTIONAL OBLIGATION.

21

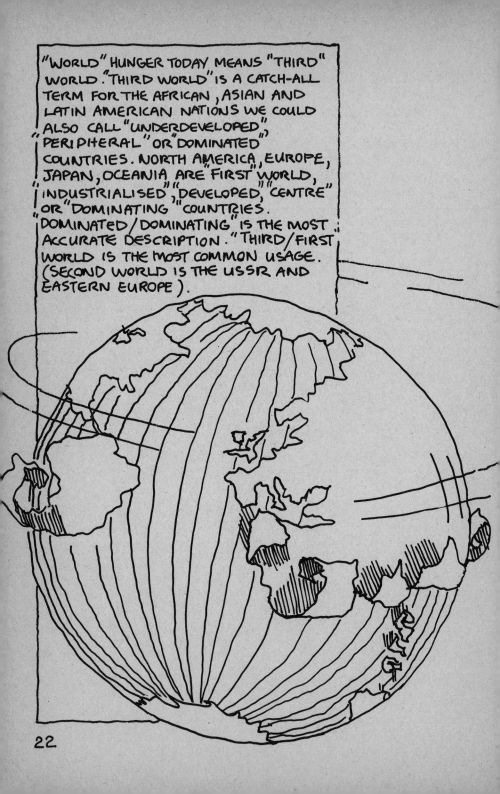

"WORLD" HUNGER TODAY MEANS "THIRD" WORLD. "THIRD WORLD" IS A CATCH-ALL TERM FOR THE AFRICAN, ASIAN AND LATIN AMERICAN NATIONS WE COULD ALSO CALL "UNDERDEVELOPED", "PERIPHERAL" OR "DOMINATED" COUNTRIES. NORTH AMERICA, EUROPE, JAPAN, OCEANIA ARE FIRST WORLD, "INDUSTRIALISED", "DEVELOPED, "CENTRE" OR "DOMINATING" COUNTRIES. "DOMINATED/DOMINATING" IS THE MOST ACCURATE DESCRIPTION. "THIRD/FIRST WORLD IS THE MOST COMMON USAGE. (SECOND WORLD IS THE USSR AND EASTERN EUROPE).

The Third World has not always had a monopoly on hunger. Europeans were not much better off in the fairly recent past. Until their own struggles and certain other factors we'll list changed the situation, their obligations to the holders of economic and political power were often overwhelming.

In Eastern Europe, the peasant had to work free for his landlord
1 day a week in 1520
3 days a week in 1550
6 days a week in 1600

In places like Silesia, a law of 1798 stipulated: "There are no limits to the work days that may be required."

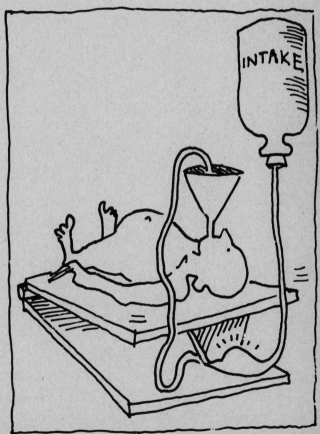

If there was no law, indebtedness would do as well. Peasants borrowed cash or food from the landlord, then had to pay it back in labour, with interest. They usually stayed on this debt treadmill all their lives.

Between ten percent and two-thirds of the peasant's own harvest was due the landlord. The lord also got his cut when the peasant brought his grain to be milled (the landlord owned the mill) or his bread to be baked (the landlord owned the oven.) In parts of Europe it was illegal to mill your own grain, bake your own bread or press your own grapes.

Cash taxes could be direct or indirect (e.g. on salt), payable to the King, the landlord or, sometimes, the Church.

So the peasant had a lot to contend with. In Pre-Revolutionary France he had about ten different obligations to the holders of political and economic power.

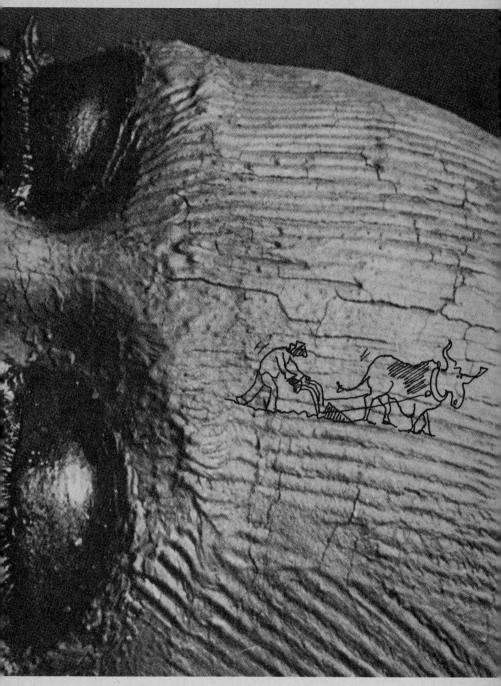

WE SHOULDN'T FORGET THE HOLDERS OF MILITARY POWER EITHER. SOLDIERS WERE NOT FED BY THOSE WHO EMPLOYED THEM BUT WERE EXPECTED TO LIVE "OFF THE LAND".

THEY OFTEN PRACTICED A SCORCHED EARTH POLICY TO PREVENT THE ENEMY FROM CAPTURING THE HARVEST.

EUROPEAN HISTORY IS FULL OF PEASANT REVOLTS, MOST OF WHICH WERE BRUTALLY PUT DOWN BY THE AUTHORITIES AFTER A FEW DAYS OR WEEKS.

27

5 Famine

ONE OF THE LAST GREAT EUROPEAN FAMINES HAPPENED IN IRELAND FROM 1846—1850. THE POTATO CROP (OUR STAPLE FOOD) WAS DEVASTATED BY BLIGHT. THAT WAS A "NATURAL" DISASTER. BUT THE DEATH BY STARVATION OF ABOUT TWO MILLION PEOPLE WAS NOT.

THE LITTLE BEGGAR KIT.

INCLUDES BOWL 2 SETS OF CLOTHES

During the famine, there was enough food inside Ireland to feed **twice** the actual population of eight million and huge exports of wheat, oats, barley, cattle, pigs, eggs and butter continued routinely. Wheat, oats and barley were, however, what we'd call today "cashcrops" grown for export and profit. The Irish peasant never ate them but grew them for the landlord. Why? Because his rent came first — even if his children were crying from hunger. Non-payment of rent meant certain eviction and a death sentence to slow starvation, for alternative wage-labour was virtually non-existant.

Competition for land was fierce and rents commonly 80-100% higher than in England. During one famine year £6,000,000 was remitted to England from Ireland, but almost nothing was reinvested by landlords.

Holdings were divided, subdivided — often by parents who could scarcely turn their children out to starve. At least half the holdings were under five acres, and thousands so small they weren't even counted in the census. Nonetheless, people kept on having lots of children as their only insurance against destitution in old age.

Even in "good" years, the Irish often went hungry during the lean summer season before the new potatoes came in and had to borrow from the dreaded "gombeen man" — the local usurer — to tide them over. The successive potato blights of 1846 and 1848 exacerbated all the injustices and hardships of "normal" times. Hungry people ate their seed potatoes, so had little to plant the following season. Landlords or their stewards got rid of tenants unable to pay their rents and razed their cottages.

6 Emigration

The price of the little food available rose astronomically, but few people were employed, even on hastily conceived public works, so they couldn't buy it. They pawned their few possessions, lived on grass or weeds as long as they could, then died — in roadside ditches if they had been turned out. Little food aid came from the British government which preferred to rely on private enterprise and the workings of the "free market". Though some money was raised privately for famine relief, there were insuperable logistical problems of distribution. When the wretched Irish showed the least signs of revolt, the government sent in not food but more troops (who also protected the food exports). Of those Irish who remained able bodied, over a million emigrated to America, and as many to England, Scotland or Wales.

34

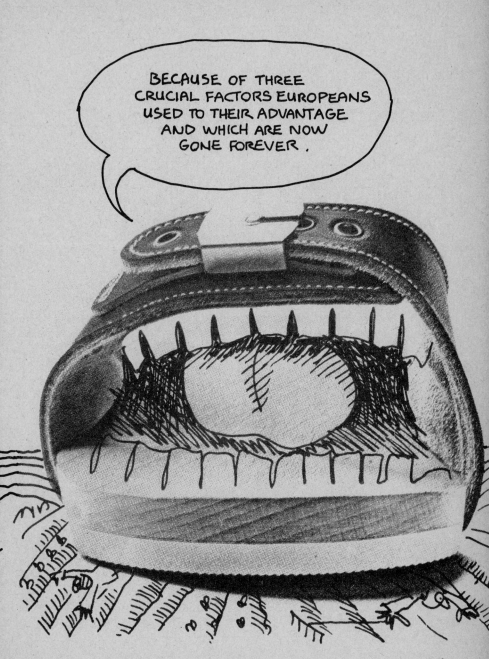

1 THE INDUSTRIAL REVOLUTION

FROM THE 18TH CENTURY, JOBS WERE BECOMING AVAILABLE IN NEW INDUSTRIES. YOU COULD SAY, IN FACT, THAT PEASANTS WERE ELIMINATED IN ORDER TO PROVIDE A PLENTIFUL AND CHEAP INDUSTRIAL LABOUR FORCE. MINES USED MORE HUMAN LABOUR THAN MACHINERY. NEW FACTORIES AND MILLS USED MACHINES, YES, BUT THEY NEEDED LOTS OF HANDS TO TEND THEM. MODERN TECHNOLOGY USES MUCH LESS LABOUR TO SERVICE IT, AND IT'S MODERN TECHNOLOGY --- THE ONLY KIND AVAILABLE -- --- THAT THE THIRD WORLD IS IMPORTING FOR ITS INDUSTRIES.

MEANWHILE THE NOW-DEVELOPED COUNTRIES HAVE AN ENORMOUS HEAD-START, AND IT IS THEIR INDUSTRIAL GOODS THAT SUPPLY 93% OF THE WORLD MARKET. THESE COUNTRIES ALSO ERECT TARIFF BARRIERS AGAINST THIRD WORLD MANUFACTURES. SO INDUSTRY IN THE POOR COUNTRIES DOESN'T CREATE ANYTHING LIKE ENOUGH JOBS FOR THE ESTIMATED 350 MILLION PEOPLE WHO NEED THEM. JOBLESS PEOPLE, WITH NO INCOME, ARE HUNGRY PEOPLE. THE CITIES CAN'T ABSORB THE DISPLACED RURAL POPULATION IN SUFFICIENT NUMBERS.

MIGRATION

Migration. About two million destitute Irish went somewhere else to try to make a new life. From 1846 to 1932, over 50 million Europeans emigrated (more than half went to the US). Places like America and Australia, Algeria and Argentina, Canada and Southern Africa provided safety valves for Europe. Today there are no new frontiers.

The emigration that now takes place from the
Third World to the First benefits the rich.
Migrant workers do dirty but necessary jobs for
low pay. The brain-drain supplies industrialised
countries with Third World-trained doctors,
engineers and technicians. This concentrates
even more know-how in the rich nations.

3 COLONIALISM

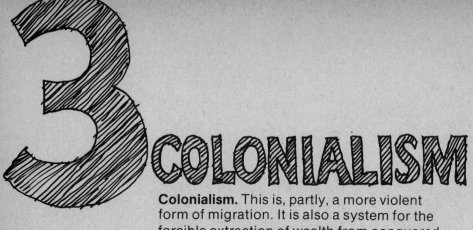

Colonialism. This is, partly, a more violent form of migration. It is also a system for the forcible extraction of wealth from conquered peoples. Naturally, there were food shortages and famines in today's poor countries before the Europeans came. Local peasants had princes, landlords and chieftains of their own to contend with. They also had, just as Europeans had for centuries, problems of low productivity that could leave them vulnerable to bad weather or blight or locusts. But pre-colonial famines do not generally seem to have had the severity or scope of "modern" ones.

Paternalism played a role. Powerholders couldn't let their dependents starve, if only because they needed them to get in the next harvest. Dependency thus worked both ways and could help at least some of the poor in lean times.

EUROPEAN TRAVELLERS OF THE 16th TO 18th CENTURIES OFTEN RETURNED FROM THEIR JOURNEYS TO WHAT IS NOW THE "THIRD WORLD" DAZZLED BY THE FOOD ABUNDANCE THEY HAD WITNESSED.

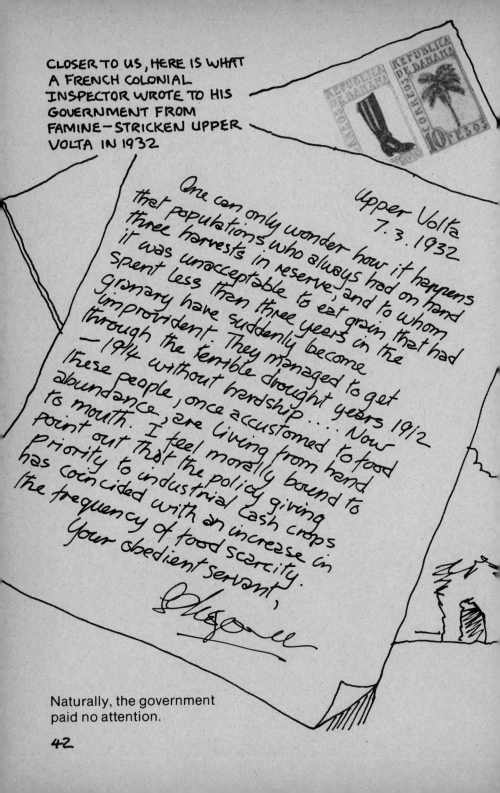

CLOSER TO US, HERE IS WHAT A FRENCH COLONIAL INSPECTOR WROTE TO HIS GOVERNMENT FROM FAMINE–STRICKEN UPPER VOLTA IN 1932

Upper Volta
7.3.1932

One can only wonder how it happens that populations who always had on hand three harvests in reserve, and to whom it was unacceptable to eat grain that had spent less than three years in the granary have suddenly become improvident. They managed to get through the terrible drought years 1912 — 1914 without hardship.... Now these people, once accustomed to food abundance, are living from hand to mouth. I feel morally bound to point out that the policy giving priority to industrial cash crops has coincided with an increase in the frequency of food scarcity.

Your obedient servant,

Naturally, the government paid no attention.

But the Inspector put his finger on one of the chief causes of hunger. Not drought, or hail, or locusts — periodic hazards the people expected and planned for — but the power to force one country to devote its resources to producing crops (or raw materials) for another. That's what colonialism is about.

You could call it the game of crops and robbers.
The French Connection — or the Spanish, Portuguese, British, Belgian, American, Italian or German one — meant that people now had to cope with the "holders of political and economic power" at the international level as well.

The colonial powers wanted raw materials for their industries. In the early 20th century, the British Peruvian Amazon Company forced thousands of Indians to collect and carry rubber to river stations. To make them work, they were driven off their subsistence plots and made dependent on food imported by the company. Thousands died of hunger (and murder).

In the Belgian Congo, finance companies expropriated millions of hectares, burned the Africans' villages and forced them to grow and gather plantation crops at gunpoint. Such companies were the ancestors of today's transnationals.

The mother countries also wanted cheap or free labour to cultivate their cash crops. If there was not enough available locally, they could ship it in. The slave-trade fuelled Caribbean sugar plantations and provided the man/woman power necessary for the US cotton-growing south.

THE FRENCH WERE MORE DEVIOUS IN THEIR METHODS. WHY USE MANPOWER TO BURN VILLAGES AND COERCE LABOUR? WHY GO TO THE EXPENSE OF PLANTATIONS WHEN YOU CAN MAKE THE NATIVES WORK FOR YOU ON THEIR OWN LAND? TAXATION WAS THE ANSWER. IF PEOPLE DIDN'T PAY THEIR TAXES YOU COULD ALWAYS, THEN, PUT THEM IN PRISON OR FORCED LABOUR GANGS. THAT WAS THEIR PROBLEM.

French reasoning: The African grows millet and sorgho. Millet and sorgho are of no interest whatever to French industry. Therefore the African must grow peanuts and cotton, which are. These he can sell, for a very low price, directly to our firms' representatives.

With this income he can pay his taxes.

Thus he can support the entire cost of our own colonial Administration and Army.

These taxes were **fixed**, not proportional and in **cash**. That is, the most burdensome kind of obligation for the peasant. Note the beauty and symmetry of a system which introduces **money** into societies which previously used it very little, if at all.

The French print the money.

The African has to earn it from the French.

The money returns to the French via taxes.

NEAT!

CONVERSATION BETWEEN A FRENCH ADMINISTRATIVE SUBORDINATE AND GOVERNOR BLACHER OF NIGER, 1931:

THERE'S A TERRIBLE FAMINE IN MY DISTRICT. PEOPLE ARE LIVING ON GRASSES AND HAVE NO MONEY FOR TAXES.

I WISH YOU TO BE LESS LENIENT AND ON THE CONTRARY, EXPECT YOU TO HASTEN THE COLLECTION OF TAXES OWED BY THOSE UNDER YOUR JURISDICTION

GOVERNOR

Able-bodied men also had to work on **corvees** — a set number of days a year — often when they should have been doing farm work. Many also had to emigrate to find wage labour to pay their taxes.

No wonder storehouses were soon emptied and chronic hunger resulted. Famine was no excuse, however, for not paying taxes.

The British had a system in India as neat as the one the French devised for Africa. They, too, wanted taxes and used the local gentry as tax-collectors (the **Zamindari** — literally "earth-holders" in Hindi.) They owed the British Raj a set sum every year. The Zamindari, in turn, named underlings, who named other under-lings, etc. right down to the peasant. In some areas, scholars have counted up to 40 inter-mediaries between the lowliest peasant and the Viceroy.

The trick was that each intermediary could keep any money over and above the sum he owed to the man immediately above him — so all had an incentive to extort the maximum.

The British also destroyed the Indian textile industry by flooding the market with British cotton goods, while requiring India to export its raw cotton.

What makes a "cash crop" is who eats or uses it. Eaters and users are **not** the producers. After the opening of the Suez Canal, India began exporting wheat to Britain. During the three terrible famine years of 1876-79 during which about six million people died, three and 3/4 million tonnes of grain were shipped out. Many individuals who served in the colonies were competent, devoted, good people with a sincere desire to "take up the white man's burden" and help the natives. But the **system** they served had the net effect of impoverishing these countries and hampering their development. The mother countries became rich at their expense and left them with a food problem.

SOMETIMES THE MOTHER COUNTRIES WANTED NOT INDUSTRIAL CROPS BUT FOOD.

TODAY, POLITICAL COLONIALISM IS NEARLY DEAD. EITHER THE MOTHER COUNTRIES GRANTED INDEPENDENCE OR NATIONAL LIBERATION MOVEMENTS FOUGHT FOR IT AND WON. BUT ECONOMIC COLONIALISM LIVES ON. ITS EFFECTS ON PEOPLES' DIETS ARE STILL DISASTROUS. IN MANY FORMER COLONIES, THE NEW LEADERS, USUALLY EDUCATED IN AND BY THE MOTHER COUNTRIES, HAVE MADE NO EFFORTS TO CHANGE COLONIAL CROP PATTERNS.

THUS SENEGAL STILL DEVOTES OVER HALF ITS ARABLE LAND TO PEANUTS AND THE PHILIPPINES GROW COCONUT OIL-PALMS AND SUGAR ON OVER HALF THEIR CROPLAND.

WHAT HAPPENS WHEN A STILL-DOMINATED COUNTRY DEPENDS ON JUST ONE OR TWO CASH CROPS FOR MOST OF ITS INCOME IN HARD CURRENCY? SUGAR-CANE, COFFEE, TEA, COCOA, ETC. ARE GROWN IN POOR COUNTRIES, BUT THE PRICES THESE CROPS FETCH ARE SET ON RICH COUNTRY COMMODITIES MARKETS. INDIVIDUAL PRODUCING COUNTRIES HAVE NO CONTROL OVER WORLD PRICES WHICH ARE VULNERABLE TO SPECULATION.

The Roller-coaster Principle

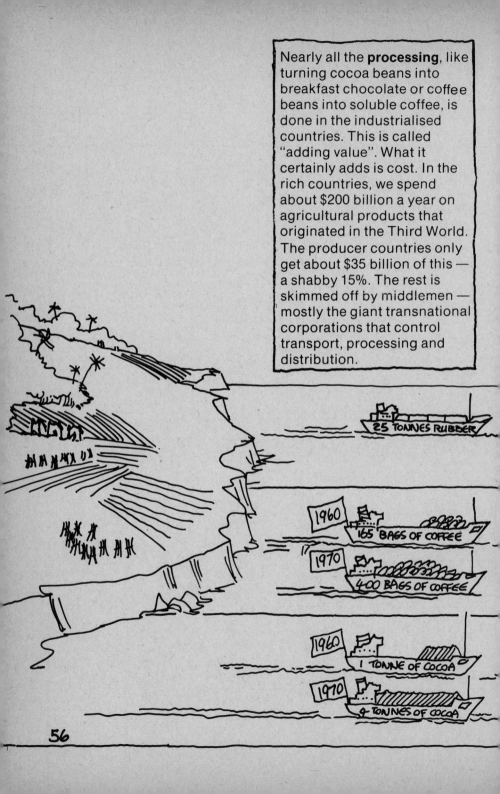

Nearly all the **processing**, like turning cocoa beans into breakfast chocolate or coffee beans into soluble coffee, is done in the industrialised countries. This is called "adding value". What it certainly adds is cost. In the rich countries, we spend about $200 billion a year on agricultural products that originated in the Third World. The producer countries only get about $35 billion of this — a shabby 15%. The rest is skimmed off by middlemen — mostly the giant transnational corporations that control transport, processing and distribution.

25 TONNES RUBBER

1960
165 BAGS OF COFFEE

1970
400 BAGS OF COFFEE

1960
1 TONNE OF COCOA

1970
4 TONNES OF COCOA

MEANWHILE, THE PRICES RICH COUNTRIES CHARGE FOR INDUSTRIAL GOODS KEEP GOING UP. THERE'S ANOTHER WORD FOR IT :

INFLATION.

50 50 50 50 50 50 1960
6 TRACTORS

50 50 1975
2 TRACTORS

50
1 TRACTOR

1200 KGS CEMENT

HOW ARE THIRD WORLD GOVERNMENTS SHARING OUT THE
REVENUES FROM CASH CROP COFFEE, COCOA OR COCONUTS?
DOES SOME OF THIS WEALTH GO INTO TRACTORS AND CEMENT
FOR EVERYONE'S BENEFIT? OR INTO MERCEDES AUTOMOBILES
AND CHAMPAGNE? ALL YOU CAN DO WITH CHAMPAGNE IS
DRINK IT. THAT IS CONSUME IT. LARGE CHUNKS OF MANY
THIRD WORLD BUDGETS GO TO CONSUMER RATHER THAN
CAPITAL GOODS (i.e., PRODUCTS WHICH CAN BE USED TO
CREATE SOMETHING ELSE.)

WHAT ABOUT THE PEASANTS WHOSE LABOUR PRODUCES CASH
CROPS — AND THE POOREST OF THEM, THE HUNGRY?

IN PLACES LIKE BRAZIL, THE RICHEST 10% GET OVER HALF OF
ALL HOUSEHOLD INCOMES, LEAVING SOME 2 OR 3% FOR
THE POOREST 20%. IN THE SOMEWHAT LESS EXTREME
CASE OF INDIA, THE TOP 10% OF HOUSEHOLDS GET 35%;
THE LOWEST 20% GET 6% OF INCOMES.

MOST OF THE THIRD WORLD'S ENERGIES ARE GOING INTO CASH CROPS, THEIR OWN FOOD CROPS ARE NEGLECTED. WHAT'S MORE, VALUE IS TAKEN FROM THE COUNTRYSIDE (IN THE FORM OF AGRICULTURAL PRODUCE) AND RETURNS TO THE CITIES (AS IMPORTS FOR THE WEALTHY) OR EVEN FOR "DEVELOPMENT" PROJECTS LIKE HOSPITALS THAT BENEFIT ONLY CITY DWELLERS.

Importing Starvation

With little investment in agriculture, yields are reduced and few jobs are created. No job = no money = no food. Since food crops are neglected, shortages soon occur. No government can simply ignore them. It must feed at least some people (especially the ones who live in cities.) Rioting mobs are known to be dangerous for a government's health.

Food imports become imperative. The big cereal exporters like Canada, Australia and France are only too happy to oblige with grain, for a price. The US, the biggest of all, is the happiest, since fully 20% of all its trade revenues come from agricultural exports. Uncle Sam has every interest in keeping both volume and prices of his food exports as high as he can.

Repression is another answer in times of scarcity — and governments know it.

In 1973, thirteen countries which had recently suffered serious food shortages were **all** devoting at least twice as much to "defense" (including police) as to investment in agriculture.

IN 1980—81 UNDERDEVELOPED COUNTRIES IMPORTED 100 MILLION TONS OF CEREALS, COMPARED TO 30 MILLION TONS 15 YEARS EARLIER. EVEN THAT LEVEL OF IMPORTS HAS LEFT MILLIONS OF PEOPLE STARVING, ESPECIALLY IN THE COUNTRYSIDE.

60

61

The Substitute Racket

There's another good reason for not relying on cash crops for national livelihood. Rich countries' industries (the transnational corporations that process and sell foods) won't accept raw material prices they can't pass on to the consumer. They have developed substitutes for all kinds of tropical products. Some are already in full-scale industrial production, like super-sweet syrup from corn, replacing cane sugar. Soap and margarine manufacturers, like Unilever, can replace any oil with any other (soybean for palm or coconut) without any change in quality. Other substitutes are ready to go when the time comes. Flavour chemists know how to create the "natural" taste of coffee or chocolate in processed food products from barley, peanuts or other temperate country crops. Even if the Third World countries get higher **prices** for their commodities, they have no guarantee they can sell the same **quantities** as before.

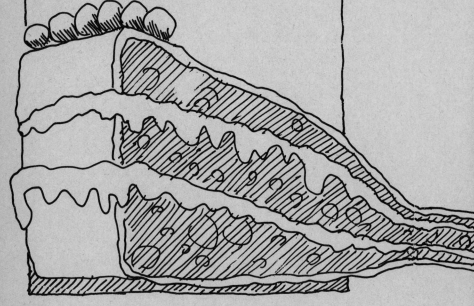

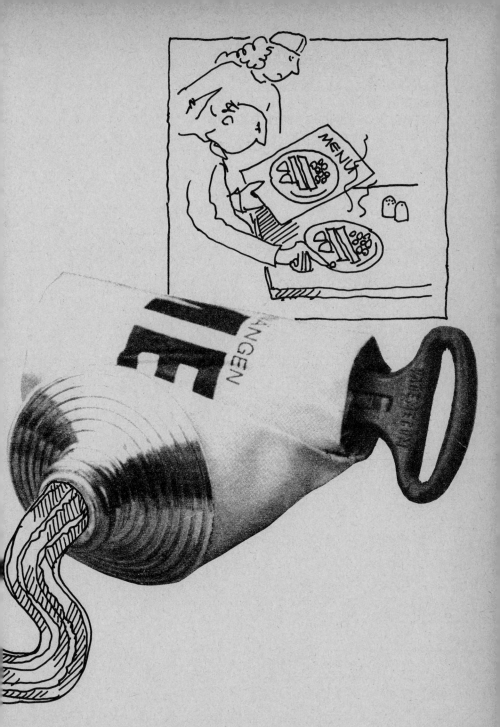

The Population Scare

THIS IS PROBABLY NOT THE WAY YOU'VE HEARD THE HUNGER STORY PRESENTED. IF YOU LIVE IN A RICH COUNTRY, YOU'VE DOUBTLESS HEARD SOMETHING ENTIRELY DIFFERENT, BECAUSE RICH COUNTRY ELITES ARE POWERFUL, BUT ALSO FRIGHTENED. OF WHAT? OF THIRD WORLD PEOPLE --- MORE SPECIFICALLY THEIR NUMBERS.

SHORT OF THERMO-NUCLEAR WAR ITSELF, POPULATION GROWTH IS THE GRAVEST ISSUE THE WORLD FACES OVER THE DECADES AHEAD. INDEED, IN MANY WAYS RAMPANT POPULATION GROWTH IS AN EVEN MORE DANGEROUS AND SUBTLE THREAT TO THE WORLD THAN THERMO-NUCLEAR WAR

THESE CURRENT POPULATION FIGURES ARE STAGGERING AND I THINK THEY DO INDICATE A POTENTIALLY EXPLOSIVE CONDITION OF SOCIAL AND POLITICAL TURBULENCE, WITH RISING POLITICAL DEMANDS & INCREASING DISSATISFACTION WITH THE STATUS QUO.

ROBERT MCNAMARA, PRESIDENT OF THE WORLD BANK UNTIL 1981

ZBIGNIEW BRZEZINSKI DECEMBER 20, 1977

DR. NORMAN BORLAUG, FATHER OF THE "GREEN REVOLUTION".

The Neo-Malthusians

Such views on population are often called "malthusian", from Rev. T.R. Malthus (1766-1834) whose **Essay on the Principle of Population** pointed out that population, unchecked, increases geometrically (1, 2, 4, 8 etc.) whereas food production can only increase arithmetically (1, 2, 3, 4 etc.). The former will therefore always tend to outstrip the latter, but it will be 'checked' by disease, war, famine and other calamities, affecting especially the poorer classes.

Malthus, no longer much read, has been criticised for a lot of things he never actually said.

Certainly he was a conservative and a defender of private property; but he came out against luxury goods for the rich as unproductive. "The present great inequality of property (which) is neither necessary nor useful to society. On the contrary, it must certainly be considered as an evil."

He also supported public investment in agriculture for provision of both food and employment and saw that demand for fewer available labourers "would better the condition of the poor . . . a labourer might then support his wife and family as well by the labour of six hours as he could before by the labour of eight".

Malthus never advocated controlling population so the rich could accumulate **more**. He hoped to improve the lot of the working poor by convincing them to reduce their numbers through "moral restraint".

Messrs. McNamara, Brzezinski, Borlaug and hundreds of others like them are not, therefore, really "malthusians". They are scared. They fear too many miserable people may make "political demands" which cannot be satisfied without basic changes in present wealth and power distribution — or start a revolutionary chain reaction which could touch even the rich countries.

67

We have all heard that **over-population** is the cause of hunger. But how many, exactly, is **over-** population? **Over** in relation to what? In relation to some ideal level where available resources, including food, are "in balance" with the number of people who want to consume them.

Aha! But who, then, is consuming the "available resources"? The United States, with 6% of world population, appears to need 35% of them. Inhabitants of the poorest countries each consume 1% as much energy yearly as an American. The rich countries as a whole (25% of world population) eat two-thirds of the world's food production. Their **animals** eat one-third of all the grains produced in the world.

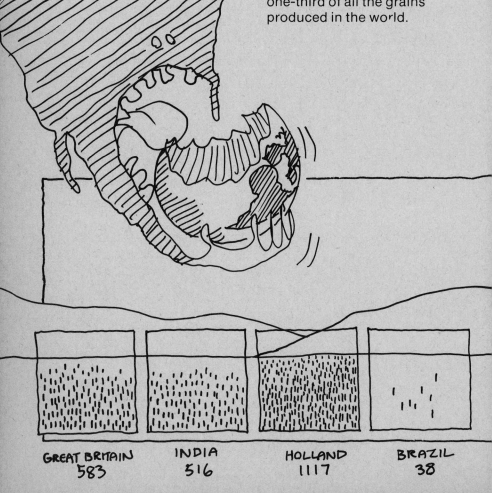

GREAT BRITAIN
583

INDIA
516

HOLLAND
1117

BRAZIL
38

More interesting facts. China, before 1949, had 500 million people and wealth concentrated in very few hands. It had famines somewhere nearly every year. China today, after the revolution, has one billion people, state farms, communes and private plots. Its population is adequately if not luxuriously fed.

Also interesting. China has only half as much arable land per person as India. No hunger, either, in Taiwan or South Korea which have only half as much arable land per person as Bangladesh and Indonesia.

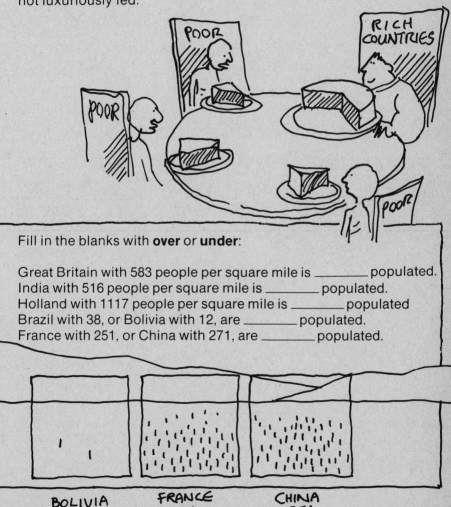

Fill in the blanks with **over** or **under**:

Great Britain with 583 people per square mile is _____ populated.
India with 516 people per square mile is _____ populated.
Holland with 1117 people per square mile is _____ populated
Brazil with 38, or Bolivia with 12, are _____ populated.
France with 251, or China with 271, are _____ populated.

BOLIVIA
12

FRANCE
251

CHINA
271

Birth Control?

Concentration of land in few hands and insecurity of tenure severely limit the amount of food that can be produced. So the obvious solution for those in power is to try to keep the population down to a level that can be **accommodated by existing unjust land-tenure structures**. This helps to explain their huge contributions to population-control programmes. They never acknowledge that people are not just mouths and stomachs, but hands and minds as well, able to improve and increase food and other kinds of production, given a chance. Historically, population growth has often resulted in "great leaps forward" in science, technology and production.

IT'S BIRTH CONTROL

IT'S A COMBINED FOOD HAND-OUT AND BIRTH CONTROL PILL.

HOW DO THIRD WORLD PARENTS LOOK AT CHILDREN? THEY NEED THEM.

AS EXTRA LABOUR. FROM A VERY YOUNG AGE KIDS CONTRIBUTE TO FAMILY LIVELIHOOD

FOR SECURITY IN OLD AGE.

AND THEY MUST PLAN TO HAVE MORE THAN THEY WANT IN THE END, BECAUSE SO MANY CHILDREN DIE BETWEEN 0-5 YEARS

POPULATION GROWTH RATES GO DOWN WHEN PEOPLE HAVE SOME SECURITY AND ACCESS TO LAND.

Naturally, women (and men) should have access to effective family-planning. Many husbands in this world still want more children (especially sons) than their wives do.
Lower birth-rates would take some pressure off present food supplies. But that wouldn't eliminate our problems. Population growth can **aggravate** hunger, but doesn't **cause** it.

FAMILY PLANNING

THEN WHAT DOES? BAD WEATHER, SOIL EROSION, SPREADING DESERTS AND OTHER NATURAL PHENOMENA? AREN'T THEY AT LEAST AS IMPORTANT AS POWER RELATIONS?

It's true, many places in the tropics have fragile ecosystems where one needs to take special precautions. But the point to remember is that people who live as part of these systems know that perfectly well. Over the centuries, they have learned to use them rationally, and that's how they've survived. A desert, for instance, may look inhospitable to you, but pastoralists (nomadic herders) know how to cope with it to their advantage. **Knowledge** of the environment is what counts.

WHAT EXACTLY CAUSES HUNGER?

NO FOOD

THE TROPICS MAY BE TOUGH, BUT THEY APPEAR VERY ATTRACTIVE INDEED TO SOME OF OUR MODERN AGRIBUSINESS MEN.

I HAVE BEEN IN PLACES WHERE TEST PLOTS WITH MULTIPLE CROPS WILL PRODUCE THREE, FOUR AND FIVE TIMES AS MUCH AS THE BEST LAND IN THE US. WHEN YOU HAVE 360 DAYS OF SUNSHINE TO WORK IN AND YOU KNOW WHAT YOU'RE DOING, THEN NEW SEEDS, PESTICIDES, CHEMICALS AND FERTILISERS CAN GIVE YOU AN EXPLOSION OF PRODUCTION.

Making Marginals

Clearly, tropical environments must have **something** going for them. The problem for many Third World peasants is that they are **no longer able** to use these environments in the traditional ways that ensured their protection. For one thing, cash crops — or rich farmers, or foreigners — tend to occupy the richest, best, flattest land. Poor farmers and herders (the majority) are pushed onto hillsides or other marginally productive land. They are then accused of "over-cultivating" or "over-grazing" it, as indeed they must if they hope to survive. There's that word again. "Over" in relation to what? To the small amount of land peasants are allowed to use.

CASH CROP KEEP OUT

4% OF THE WORD'S BIG LANDOWNERS CONTROL HALF THE WORLDS CROPLAND (JUST 0.23% OF OWNERS CONTROL OVER HALF OF ALL LAND, CROP OR OTHERWISE, WORLDWIDE).
UNEQUAL DISTRIBUTION IS NOT RESERVED FOR THE THIRD WORLD. IN THE USA, 5% OF THE FARMERS WORK OVER HALF THE CROPLAND.

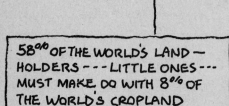

58% OF THE WORLD'S LANDHOLDERS - - - LITTLE ONES - - - MUST MAKE DO WITH 8% OF THE WORLD'S CROPLAND

IN 83 POOR COUNTRIES, 3% OF THE LANDHOLDERS OWN OR CONTROL FOUR-FIFTHS OF THE LAND.

NOT TO MENTION THAT IN MANY COUNTRIES, ESPECIALLY IN ASIA, A THIRD TO A HALF OF THE RURAL POPULATION HAS NO LAND AT ALL. THAT'S TRUE IN JAVA, BANGLADESH, MANY PARTS OF INDIA, BUT ALSO EGYPT, VENEZUELA, MEXICO, ETC.

Even with all these disadvantages, small farmers in most places produce more food per acre than large ones. Lots of vast holdings are underused or not used at all. Latin America is a big offender here. One study showed that in Brazil, Argentina and Chile, small family farms produced over 8 times as much to the acre as the largest 'latifundia'. In Colombia, the efficiency of small farms was a stunning 14 times greater. That's because small farmers give the land everything they've got — mostly labour. But such productivity isn't possible where the land quality has decreased.

IN AFRICA, THE LAND SQUEEZE ON PEASANTS HAS RESULTED IN REDUCED FALLOW PERIODS, WHERE THE LAND USED TO "REST" UP TO 10 YEARS OR SO, AND THIS LOWERS YIELDS. MILLIONS OF SMALL SHARECROPPERS AND TENANTS COULD, HOWEVER, PRODUCE A LOT MORE THAN THEY DO. SO WHY DON'T THEY? BECAUSE THEY HAVE TO PAY FOR ALL IMPROVEMENTS AND INPUTS (FERTILISER, IRRIGATION, ETC.), BUT THE LANDLORD GETS MOST OF THE BENEFITS. THIS IS OBVIOUS WHEN RENT DUE IS PROPORTIONAL/KIND.

BUT IT WORKS THAT WAY EVEN WHEN RENT IS FIXED. HERE'S HOW IT WORKS IN THE INDIAN STATE OF TAMIL NADU. HALF THE LAND THERE IS FARMED UNDER TENANCY. THE LANDOWNER GETS A FIXED/KIND RENT (ABOUT 50-60% OF THE AVERAGE HARVEST). SHARECROPPING (PROPORTIONAL/KIND) ISN'T PRACTICED BECAUSE MOST LANDLORDS ARE ABSENTEE AND IN NO POSITION TO KEEP AN EYE ON THE VOLUME OF THE HARVEST. YOU WOULD THINK TENANTS WOULD TRY AND INCREASE VOLUME BECAUSE THIER RENT IS FIXED.

SO HE DOESN'T WORK ON HIS OWN LAND

BUT NO. HIGH RENTS KEEP
TENANTS FROM
ACCUMULATING SAVINGS.
SO THEY HAVE NO CASH TO
INVEST IN PURCHASED
INPUTS. THEY CAN BORROW
VERY LITTLE FROM OFFICIAL
CREDIT SOURCES. THE ONLY
ALTERNATIVE FOR CREDIT IS
THE MONEY LENDER AT A
MINIMUM 6% A MONTH.
CAPITAL, FOR THE TENANT,
COSTS MUCH MORE THAN IT
DOES FOR THE LANDOWNER.
INTEREST ON THE DEBT
WOULD EAT UP THE WHOLE
PRODUCT OF AN EXTRA
HARVEST. TENANTS ARE
BETTER OFF SELLING THEIR
LABOUR IRREGULARLY
THAN INVESTING IN INPUTS
OR IN A SECOND CROP.
THEY MAKE PERFECTLY
RATIONAL ECONOMIC
DESISIONS BUT
OVERALL FOOD
RRODUCTION SUFFERS.

BANK
BARTER
POINT

SQUAWK

Lots of people blame "climate" or "drought" for the Third World's food problem. There's no doubt that sharp variations in the weather hit producers hard. But they don't suffer equally, and some even profit from bad weather. To understand how this happens, we can use

SPITZ'S LAW

Pierre Spitz's model of the effects of drought on "self-provisioning". "Spitz's Law" is easy to remember: "In capitalist ("free market") economies, Self Provisioning Intensity Tends to Zero". Get it? The way the weather hits people is directly related to their relative economic strength. This strength, or weakness, is based on two factors quite foreign to people living in rich countries (and in cities).

First, in industrialised societies, there are practically no farmers left who make their own bread from their own wheat. They sell their wheat and then buy their bread from a shop, like everyone else. In other words, these farmers live in a wholly "monetised" economy. Everything has cash value and is exchanged through the medium of money. We tend to forget that in poor countries, peasants produce first and foremost for their own family consumption. If part of the harvest is left over, so much the better. It can be bartered or sold for cash — this is called the "marketable surplus". Third World rural families have two separate budgets: one in cash and one in kind (food, mostly).

SELF
PROVISIONING
INTENSITY
TENDS TO
ZERO

SLOW

AGRICULTURAL
INVESTMENT

Second, in rich countries, though we notice rainy or dry years, and the differences between summer and winter, we're not **dependent** on the seasons or on climatic variations. In spite of inflation, we know that our loaf of bread is going to cost approximately the same amount just after the wheat harvest and six months later, in a dry year or in a wet one. Not so for the poor peasant. If he can't grow enough food for himself and his family, he must count on the price of purchased food going steadily upwards between one harvest and the next. He knows that in a bad year, prices will go up **more**. The peasant lives from week to week, month to month, and the bases of the decisions he has to make are constantly shifting.

SUPPOSE WE WANT TO STUDY FOOD PRODUCTION AND CONSUMPTION IN AN INDIAN VILLAGE. MOST RESPECTABLE PhDs IN AGRICULTURAL ECONOMICS WOULD TELL US TO:

GET OUT INTO THE FIELDS, MEASURE THE AREA AND ASCERTAIN THE QUALITY OF EACH FAMILY'S LANDS. THESE SHOULD BE WEIGHTED WITH THE KIND OF TECHNOLOGY USED (IRRIGATION? FERTILISER?) AND THE AMOUNT OF LABOUR EMPLOYED. THESE VARIABLES SHOULD ALLOW US TO CALCULATE THE AVERAGE YIELD, FROM WHICH WE MUST BE CAREFUL TO DEDUCT THE COSTS OF TECHNOLOGY AND OF PAID LABOUR. THEN WE MUST COUNT THE NUMBER OF MOUTHS TO FEED PER FAMILY AND DETERMINE THE NECESSARY NUMBER OF KILOS OF GRAIN NEEDED FOR ADEQUATE NUTRITION, ACCORDING TO THE AGE, SEX AND WORKLOAD OF EACH FAMILY MEMBER, PER ANNUM. HAVING CALCULATED ALL THIS FOR, SAY, TWO HUNDRED FAMILIES IN THE VILLAGE, WE CAN DETERMINE THE PERCENTAGE OF FAMILIES WHOSE AVERAGE YIELDS ARE INFERIOR TO THE AMOUNT OF FOOD THEORETICALLY NECESSARY FOR THEIR PROPER NUTRITION.

GOT ANY MORE PhD'S?

FERTILIZER

If the student doesn't do all this measuring and calculating him/herself, he's supposed to question all the heads of families very closely on these matters.

Such surveys provide thesis material for advanced degree candidates and gainful employment to computer corporation personnel.

How
The Peasant Measures Output

Since families in Indian villages have little opportunity to employ computer programmers, they do not proceed in this fashion. The peasant may not even know the precise size of his plot, nor have any very clear ideas about his average yield per unit of land. This is why many PhDs consider him "backward" and "irrational".

What the peasant does know, however, to the week or the day, is **how long he was able to feed his family from his harvest**, and when he had to start making cash outlays for food. Think about it. This one piece of information **takes in** land area and quality, yield, technology, labour use, number of mouths to feed and levels of consumption per family member.

WE'VE GOT TEN ACRES OF UNIRRIGATED LAND, FIVE CHILDREN BETWEEN 8 AND 20, AND GRANNY. WE CAN PRODUCE FOR SIX MONTHS OF SELF-PROVISIONING

SO CAN WE WITH 3 ACRES OF IRRIGATED LAND, A PART-TIME HIRED HAND AND 4 CHILDREN UNDER 10.

NEITHER FAMILY NEEDS A COMPUTER. BUT THEY WILL HAVE TO MAKE THE SAME KINDS OF DIFFICULT CHOICES AND SOLVE THE SAME

PROBLEMS DURING THE COURSE OF THE YEAR, BECAUSE EACH IS CONFRONTED WITH A SIX MONTH FOOD GAP.

Spitz's Model Of Seven Families

Now let's set up a table to show how good and bad years affect different families according to their rung in the social and economic ladder. To simplify, assume that we are starting the year just after harvest and all the people in the village have paid off their obligations on the first day of the year. We'll also assume a single harvest a year and that none of the families have kept carryover stocks from the previous year. Of course, all families are **consuming** their Year One harvest and at the same time **producing** the harvest to be brought in at the end of Year Two. Year Two turns out to be a bad drought year, and every family's production goes down by one-third. The consequences of the drought will be felt in Year Three. Here's how the change in climate will hit seven typical families in our village, called:

Ali

Baba

Cool

Dark

We are dealing here **only** with families that have some land. The landless are worse off.

In many places, there may be two (occasionally even three) harvests a year. This would complicate the calendar, but not change the principle.

We are not comparing rigorously equal **quantities** because all figures are given in number of months of self-provisioning, and as we've seen, one family's consumption for the same number of months may be greater or smaller than another's. We are comparing the **situations** each one faces.

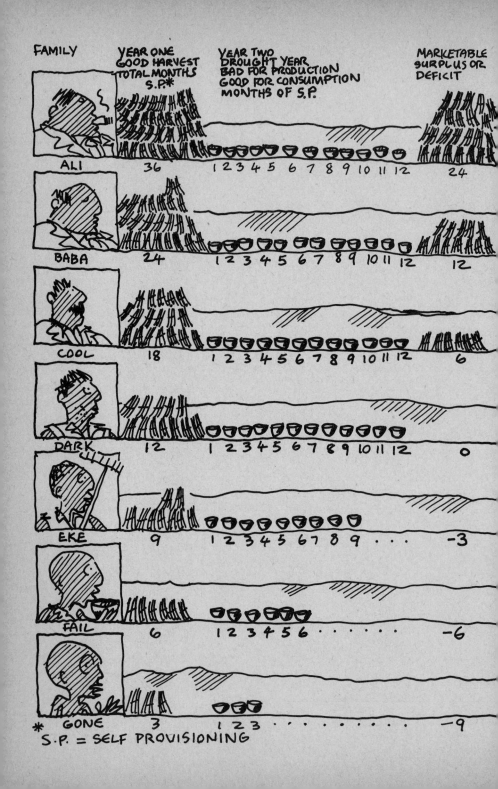

FAMILY | YEAR ONE GOOD HARVEST TOTAL MONTHS S.P.* | YEAR TWO DROUGHT YEAR BAD FOR PRODUCTION GOOD FOR CONSUMPTION MONTHS OF S.P. | MARKETABLE SURPLUS OR DEFICIT

ALI — 36 — 1 2 3 4 5 6 7 8 9 10 11 12 — 24

BABA — 24 — 1 2 3 4 5 6 7 8 9 10 11 12 — 12

COOL — 18 — 1 2 3 4 5 6 7 8 9 10 11 12 — 6

DARK — 12 — 1 2 3 4 5 6 7 8 9 10 11 12 — 0

EKE — 9 — 1 2 3 4 5 6 7 8 9 . . . — -3

FAIL — 6 — 1 2 3 4 5 6 . . . . . . — -6

GONE — 3 — 1 2 3 . . . . — -9

* S.P. = SELF PROVISIONING

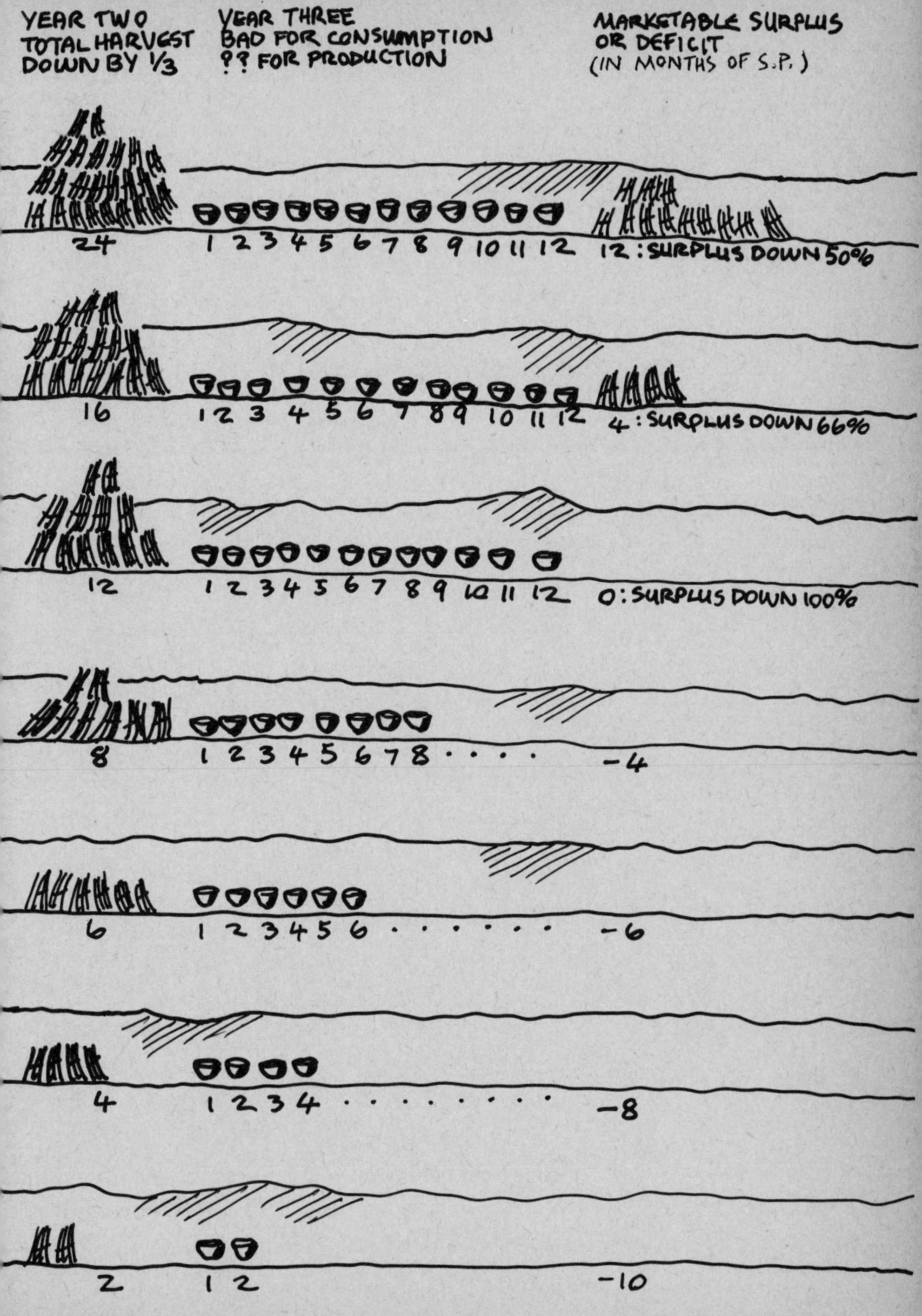

YEAR TWO
TOTAL HARVEST
DOWN BY 1/3

YEAR THREE
BAD FOR CONSUMPTION
?? FOR PRODUCTION

MARKETABLE SURPLUS
OR DEFICIT
(IN MONTHS OF S.P.)

24 · · · 1 2 3 4 5 6 7 8 9 10 11 12 · · · 12 : SURPLUS DOWN 50%

16 · · · 1 2 3 4 5 6 7 8 9 10 11 12 · · · 4 : SURPLUS DOWN 66%

12 · · · 1 2 3 4 5 6 7 8 9 10 11 12 · · · 0 : SURPLUS DOWN 100%

8 · · · 1 2 3 4 5 6 7 8 · · · · · · −4

6 · · · 1 2 3 4 5 6 · · · · · · −6

4 · · · 1 2 3 4 · · · · · · · −8

2 · · · 1 2 · · · · · · · −10

1 Ali

The wealthiest family in the village, with a total of 36 months of self-provisioning in a good year (12 + 24 of surplus). After the drought year, their marketable surplus drops by 50%. (Actually, it wouldn't drop that much because rich families have more control over water and other resources, but we're trying to keep this manageable.) But they will stay as rich and doubtless even **improve** their position. They do not have to reduce consumption after a reduced harvest. Their health will not suffer, and all

the Alis will have plenty of energy for the peak farm-work period (which starts about month 7). Moreover, even though Ali's marketable surplus has been reduced by half, he can afford to wait to sell it. The longer he waits, the higher he knows prices will go. If prices double, Ali's income will be exactly the same as in a "good" year. If prices triple, his cash income will actually rise by 50%. In a real famine year, he could make a killing as prices increased by a factor of eight to ten towards the end of month 12.

2 Baba

Situation akin to Ali's. But since Baba's surplus has been reduced by two-thirds, he may decide to cut his family's consumption in order to have more grain to sell and keep his cash income stable.

3 Cool

Cool, in the post-drought year has no surplus at all. But his family was accustomed to some money income. Cool reduces everyone's rations in order to keep on paying his son's school fees. He postpones his daughter's wedding, and buys no clothes or farm inputs in hopes of a better harvest in year three.

4 Dark

Dark can just make it in a good year. Suddenly he is confronted with the need to cut his family's consumption by a third, or find outside work. He's lucky enough to find a job right away, and buys food with his wages. He knows it's better to buy cheap now and eat his own grain later when prices will be much higher. But he's employed on someone else's land when he ought to be working his own. His year three harvest will suffer.

5 Eke

The Ekes try Dark's strategy because they will only be able to cover half a year's needs with their own produce. Ali accepts to employ Eke and Eke's son, at wages well under the going "good year" rate. He puts them to work repairing his irrigation well and digging a new one. These improvements to Ali's property cost him very little. Eke still has to borrow grain from Ali to make it through months 10 to 12. From his next meagre harvest, on day one, he'll have to pay back 1½ measures for every measure borrowed. His consumption in year three is cut drastically, but will be cut even more in year four. Eke gets so little to eat that he's often too ill and exhausted to work when plowing and sowing time comes.

6 Fail

Fail has to borrow from Ali even earlier, mortgaging his land as collateral. Where does Ali get the wherewithal to lend? Partly from his own cash reserves, but mostly from the local bank where he's a good customer. He borrows at legitimate interest-rates and re-lends at ten times the interest. Fail's daughter accepts unpaid, unlimited service, in exchange for being fed, in the Ali's scullery, making one less mouth to feed. Fail's son leaves school to look for casual work. The family's fate will depend on whether he finds it. If not, Ali may foreclose on Fail's land.

7 Gone

Gone and his family are already deeply in debt from month three. They make it barely through month six on credit and selling off cheap Mrs. Gone's remaining jewelry and Gone's bullock. Finally, Gone can get no more credit and the family literally begins to starve. As a last resort, he has to sell his land — to Ali, who buys it at several times less than its value. Without work or land, Gone goes — to the city, where we lose his trace. He may be dead by now.

NEEDLESS TO SAY, THERE ARE FAR MORE DARK, EKE, FAIL AND GONE FAMILIES IN THE THIRD WORLD COUNTRYSIDE THAN THERE ARE ALIS, BABAS OR EVEN COOLS. IF "CLIMATE" IS A BIG FACTOR IN THEIR LIVES, IT'S BECAUSE THE SUN SHINES AND THE RAIN FALLS DIFFERENTLY ON DIFFERENT SOCIAL STRATA. EVERY POOR YEAR REDUCES THE SURVIVAL CAPACITY OF FAMILIES AT THE BOTTOM OF THE LADDER.

What is Famine ?

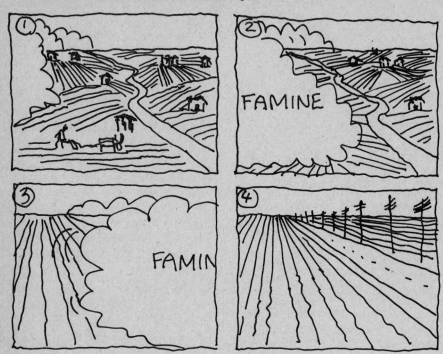

No surprise that with a lower harvest, prices rise. But note also in this case that when the **harvest** goes down by a third, the **surplus** drops by over 60% (from 42 to 16 months equivalent self-provisioning). A bad year has an effect on **prices** that is much greater, proportionally, than on **production**. This happens internationally too. In 1973, world harvests dropped by only about 2%, but world grain prices shot up to unprecedented levels, sometimes by as much as 300%.

We keep coming back to the basic, unavoidable fact. People have no power over land and income. Too little/no land; too little/no income equals hunger and sometimes physical extinction. If this condition simultaneously hits large segments of the population, what you get is called **famine**.

Every famine has its own specific causes because the relationships between the dominating/powerful and dominated/powerless classes are different in each society and historical period. A natural disaster like blight or drought can easily trigger it off. But the drought is not the basic **cause**. Lots of other factors come into play — factors against which the hungry can offer little resistance. Poor people, by definition, have very limited options. Control over food supplies, being vital in any society, is a terrain for conflict. As the conflict grows more acute, the whole society sometimes breaks down. A famine, whether in Ireland or in India, represents a major crisis in a social system. That society won't simply "go back to normal" once the crisis is past. Unless the powerless have somehow managed to take control, their situation is going to be even worse in the future. These crises have some common features.

PEOPLE MOST VUNERABLE TO
FOOD SHORTAGE HAVE :

NO CASH RESERVES :
FOOD PRICES RISE : THE FOOD
PEASANTS HAVE TO SELL CHEAP
AT HARVEST TIME, THEY MUST
BUY BACK LATER IN THE YEAR
AT EXHORBITANT COST.
SPECULATORS MAKE
FORTUNES.
MORE = INDEBTEDNESS
AFTER THE FAMINE

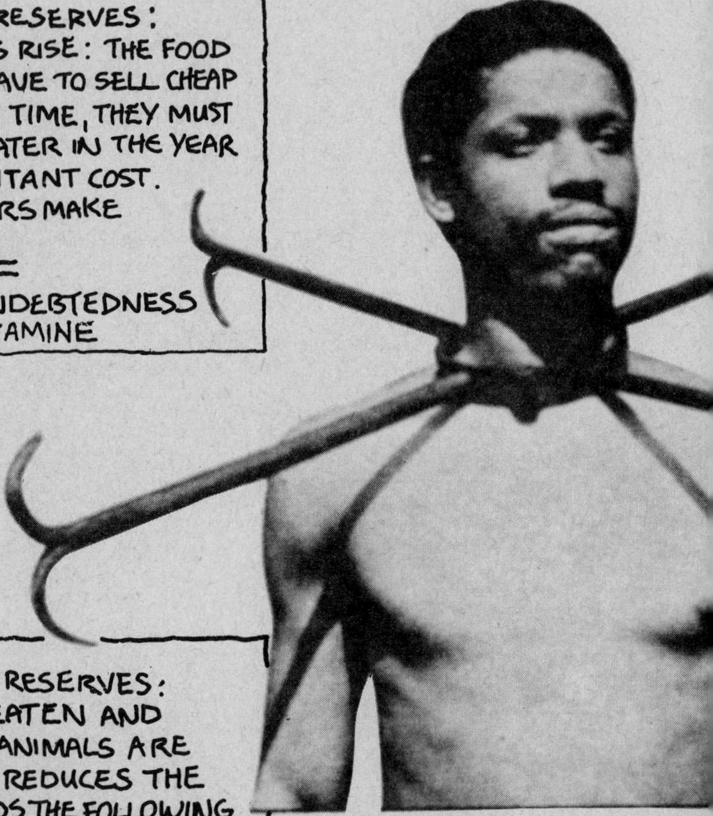

NO FOOD RESERVES :
SEEDS ARE EATEN AND
DRAUGHT ANIMALS ARE
SOLD. THIS REDUCES THE
CROP YIELDS THE FOLLOWING
YEAR . HEAVY BORROWING
ENSUES ; EQUIPMENT AND
LAND ARE MORTGAGED.
MORE = CONCENTRATION
OF LAND IN FEWER HANDS

NO SECURE TITLE TO LAND :
LANDLORDS EVICT "EXCESS" TENANTS WHO
COULD CLAIM A SHARE OF THE HARVEST. THE
WEALTHY CAN ACQUIRE AT "FAMINE PRICES" LAND
THAT SMALL PEASANTS ARE SELLING AS A LAST
RESORT IN ORDER TO BUY FOOD
=
MORE LANDLESS PEOPLE AFTER THE FAMINE

NO JOB OPPORTUNITIES :
THE NUMBER OF LANDLESS
JOBSEEKERS INCREASES. SO DOES
THE COMPETITION FOR THE FEW JOBS
AVAILABLE, SO WAGES GO DOWN IN
SPITE OF HIGHER FOOD PRICES.
=
MORE UNEMPLOYED AFTER...

NO PLACE TO GO :
EXEPT THE CITY, WHERE THEY MAY FIND A SOUP
KITCHEN IF THEY ARE LUCKY AND IF THE ARMY
DOESN'T BEAT THEM BACK
=
MORE DISPLACED RURAL MIGRANTS IN CITY
SLUMS AFTER THE FAMINE

ALL OF WHICH SETS THE STAGE FOR AN EVEN WORSE
FAMINE NEXT TIME THERE IS A NATURAL
DISASTER LIKE BLIGHT OR DROUGHT. THE RICH
HAVE GOT RICHER THE POOR MORE MARGINAL.
BOTH THE URBAN AND THE RURAL PROLETARIAT
HAVE GROWN LARGER

Harmful Interventions

Rich countries and international agencies with their "aid" programmes and "development solutions" contribute to making an already calamitous situation even worse.

They push "population control" (and dump unsafe contraceptives in Third World countries) instead of trying to change the conditions that make people **need** children.

They encourage cash-crop production and refuse most other Third World goods through trade barriers.

MOBILE MULTI NATIONAL AUDIO VISUAL PROPAGANDA UNIT

They consistently give economic, political and military support to régimes that have no intention of improving the lot of their own poor people. And they do everything to wreck the efforts of those who do strive for agrarian reform and fairer distribution (Allende's Popular Unity government in Chile, for example).

There is a more subtle and ultimately more harmful kind of intervention the West touts as a "solution", and it takes a little more explaining. Essentially, rich countries are trying to make Third World food systems resemble or serve their own. If they could manage it (which they can't, entirely, yet), the most powerful countries would set up a **single** world food-system which they controlled.

Instead of telling the dominating countries to go to hell; instead of inventing their own solutions to their own problems, most dominated countries seem to **want** to imitate rich country food systems,

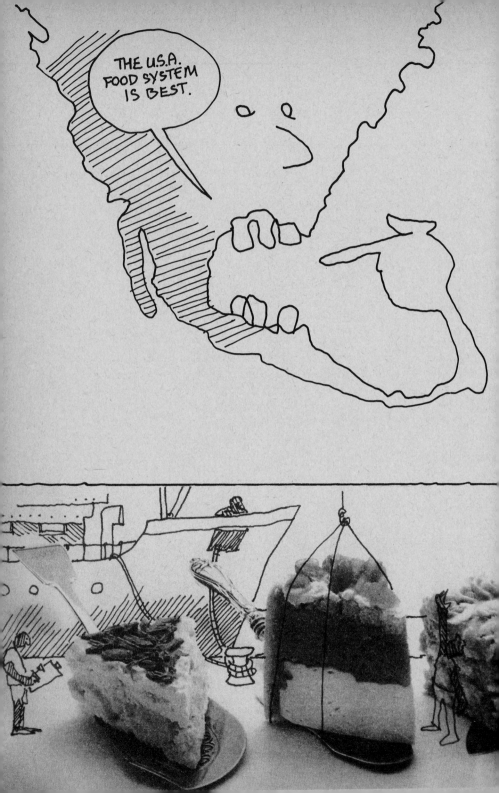

Imitation is not only the sincerest form of
flattery — it's very good for business and for
enhancing political clout as well. Europe has
already exchanged its pre-war food system for
the version made in USA. Now the vote is
unanimous. The US system is the most
Developed, the most Modern, the most
Efficient, the most Productive. The eighth
wonder of the world, in sum.
If syphilis were American, would the rest of the
world want it?
It's understandable. People admire a food
system that keeps pouring a stream of wheat,
feedgrains, soybeans and even rice from a
bottomless cornucopia onto world markets.
Where would everyone else be without this
bounty? America seems to be the bread-basket
to end all bread-baskets.
Before we join the chorus of praise, we want
to ask two pertinent or impertinent questions.
First, is this system really so Efficient, so
Productive etc?
Second, and more important in the context of
world hunger, should it be a model for the rest
of the world?
Our answer to both questions is **NO**.

What Is A Food System **?**

The reasons lie in the very nature of this food
system — and it's about time we defined that
term. A food system looks like this:

1 INPUTS.
SEEDS, MACHINERY, WATER,
FERTILIZER AND CHEMICALS
RESEARCH AND CREDIT.
EVERYTHING THAT GOES INTO
PRODUCTION.

2 AGRICULTURAL PRODUCTION.
EVERYTHING THE FARMER
OR ANIMAL RAISER DOES.

YOU CAN USE A SIMPLE MODEL LIKE THIS TO DESCRIBE THE WAY ANY COMMUNITY GOES ABOUT FEEDING ITSELF. FOR ESKIMOES, REPLACE "HARVEST" WITH "CATCH." THE RELATIVE WEIGHT OF THE THREE SECTORS WILL, HOW— EVER, CHANGE ENORMOUSLY FROM SOCIETY TO SOCIETY. IN SOME COUNTRIES, YOU MIGHT FIND TWO OR MORE MODELS; BUT ONE IS USUALLY DOMINANT AND IN THE PROCESS OF DRIVING THE OTHERS OUT.

3 POST HARVEST ACTIVITIES. STORAGE, PROCESSING DISTRIBUTION, RESTAURANTS AND MASS FEEDING: EVERYTHING THAT HAPPENS TO FOOD AFTER IT LEAVES THE FARMER UNTIL IT REACHES THE CONSUMER.

RESTAURANT

Industrial Farming

In industrialised countries, we have gradually given much more weight to sectors **one** and **three**. This means very small proportions of our populations (just 2-3% in the US or UK) are actually engaged in farming. We produce great amounts of food with few people because we devote enormous amounts of capital to inputs — like hybrid seeds and fertilisers and labour-saving machinery.

"Productivity" — the output per person — has grown faster in agriculture than in any other industry in the US throughout the 20th century. This sounds like a real success story. In many ways, and for lots of farmers, however, it's been a failure story. We have to hit you with some numbers here, because numbers convey most quickly what's happening.

The cost of inputs rises steadily. Just after World War II, US farmers spent about half their incomes on production costs (meaning inputs). Now it's over 80%. In 1979 alone, their costs went up by 14-20%, depending on the crop raised. To make using powerful machinery worthwhile, to amortise costs, farmers must try to acquire as much land as they can. They can usually do this only at the expense of smaller neighbours. So they borrow, for expansion and input purchases — in the US now about $195 billion in credit is outstanding, twice as much as in 1975. That's the good news.

The bad news is that farm incomes fell by fully 1/3 between 1979-80. Even in "good" times, US farms fail at the rate of about 700 a week. This figure is expected to double in 1981. Just a few more snappy figures and you'll have the whole picture. It now takes about $400,000 to create a single job in farming, or ten times as much as to create one in industry. Don't try to go into agriculture unless you have a pile of capital (or a father with a farm).

CONCENTRATION OF INCOME IS FANTASTIC! IN 1978 IN THE U.S. JUST 826 SUPERFARMS EARNED 10% OF ALL AGRICULTURAL RECEIPTS.

The Oligopoly Factor

The average age of a US farmer is 52. The average U S farm has grown from 278 acres in 1960 to over 400 today.

Over four million farms have gone out of business since the mid-thirties of the 2.3 million US farmers, fewer than 100,000 produce **half** of all the crops and animals. One third of the farms produce 90% of the food. The other two-thirds must find some income outside farming. The rule, in the immortal words of former Secretary of Agriculture Butz, is "Get Big or Get Out". This creates unemployment, especially for minorities (virtually no black farmers left in the U S).

Even rich farmers complain that the big companies supplying them with tractors, seeds, animals feeds, etc. are overcharging them. They're right. The government agrees and has prosecuted some companies; but trustbusting attempts have had little practical effect. Where four or fewer companies in each of the main product lines control over half the market, you get OLIGOPOLY. That's Greek for "Few Sell". When Few sell to many buyers, the Few have no reason to compete on price. Nice enough when you belong to the club. Not so nice for farmers who must meet rising costs with shrinking incomes.

ANY SUPERMARKET GIVES THE IMPRESSION OF ENORMOUS PROFUSION AND VARIETY OF GOODS. IN FACT, IN THE US, THE TOP 50 FOOD FIRMS CONTROL OVER TWO-THIRDS OF ALL THE INDUSTRY'S ASSETS. AT THEIR PRESENT RATE OF GROWTH AND MERGER, THESE 50 WILL OWN ALL FOOD MANUFACTURING ASSETS BY 2,000 AD.

THEY SELL UNDER HUNDREDS OF DIFFERENT BRAND NAMES. PUTTING THEIR REAL NAMES ON THEIR GOODS WOULD MAKE YOU REALISE THAT THE HUGE ASSORTMENT YOU'RE OFFERED IS, COMMERCIALLY SPEAKING, MUCH LESS VARIED THAN MEETS THE EYE.

COMPANIES UNDERSTAND VERY WELL THEY'RE NOT LIKELY TO MAKE MUCH MONEY SELLING PRODUCE JUST THE WAY IT COMES OFF THE FARM OR JUST BARELY TRANSFORMED, LIKE WHEAT IN THE FORM OF PLAIN MILLED FLOUR. LONG AND COSTLY PROCESSING IS THEIR STOCK IN TRADE.

Only about 8% of what supermarkets sell is fresh produce (fruits, vegetables and eggs). All the rest has gone through the companies' shiny machines. These corporations buy 90% of all the food grown for domestic use in the US for further processing. Why sell a couple of pounds of raw potatoes if you can dehydrate and rehydrate them, throw in some additives, cut them to identical shape, deep-fry them, spray on flavouring and pack them in vacuum-seal metal tennis-ball cans — at dozens of times the cost of the original, long-suffering potato? In sector three, post-harvest, there is no more competition on price than there is in sector one, inputs. Four firms, or less, control well over half the market in any food category you care to mention — bakery or dairy products, tinned fruits and vegetables, processed meats, sugar, etc.

Even the US Department of Agriculture says consumers are overcharged 10% for their whole market basket because of oligopoly in food marketing. Overcharges are much higher for products that advertising has convinced you are "different" from each other. TV and jingles can, apparently, make people willingly purchase and pay 15-20% more than they "should" (if real competition existed) for candy, chewing gum, cookies and crackers, oils and margarines, cake mixes, tinned meats, soft drinks and pet foods — and fully 30% more for breakfast cereals. In other words, the junkier it is, the more profit for the companies.

The Costs of Profit

This food system **is** efficient, but only if you're willing to measure all efficiency in terms of **profit** and not count any of the costs that do not show up on a corporate balance sheet. Some costs that don't appear on such ledgers are:

The human costs. The hundreds of farm families that have to change their way of life every week. The drying up of local markets as everything is packaged and marketed nation-wide. The slow disintegration of rural centres as more and more residents — not just farmers but shopkeepers, doctors or teachers — move away for lack of livelihood.

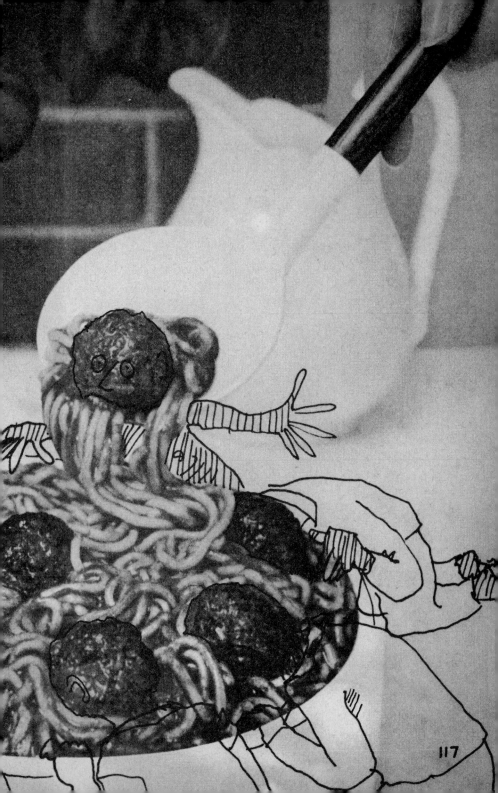

The nutritional and health costs. Eminent doctors and nutritionists have testified to the US Senate that the US health budget could be slashed by up to a third — about $70 billion — if people improved their diets. (Dentists, for instance, would lose half their clientele overnight). Lots of sugar & fat & yummy additives & marbled, grain-fed beef, MMMMMMM just the thing for heart disease, diabetes and a host of other maladies.

Still, America subsidises a system so costly that $10 billion Federal outlay on food stamps and feeding programmes is necessary if the poor are not to starve. And the poor, with their food stamps, can then buy that delicious junk food diet. Their malnourishment often shows up as obesity.

Recent reports show that in Britain, "there are clear signs that the average nutritional status of the population is falling" (in the late 70s), especially for the poor, the unemployed and the elderly. Furthermore, "the British public have very little interest in food values and their knowledge, such as it is, has virtually no influence on what they eat". It is largely advertising that determines what both Americans and British eat.

The environmental costs. Every farmer in such a system, if he wants to survive, **must** get every last ounce of produce out of the land he works. And he must get it **now**, regardless of the long-term costs. Two bushels of topsoil are currently lost in producing every bushel of corn and the US has irrevocably said goodbye to a third of its topsoil.

So many pesticides are used that they sometimes **create** pest outbreaks because they destroy natural predators. Doses of fertilisers have to be increased yearly, and yet yields of all the major crops have leveled off, or even **declined**, since the early seventies. Water is mined like it's going out of style. In another twenty years or so, major reservoirs will have disappeared at current rates of exploitation.

121

The energy costs. It takes 1400 litres of oil per American per year to keep this whole system functioning. If you wanted to feed four billion people in the world an American diet (yech!) using American methods, all the known oil reserves would be exhausted in eleven years. Energy use in this food system tripled between 1940-1970.

The genetic costs. Just a handful of varieties of every species makes up the bulk of the crop. Four Canadian breadwheats account for 75% of all production; 2 kinds of peas for 96% of the US harvest; 6 kinds of corn cover 70% of the vast corn belt. In these circumstances, if a blight hits, a huge part of the crop can be zapped (this happened to US corn in 1970) The Academy of Sciences puts it more elegantly: "US crops are impressively uniform genetically and impressively vulnerable". Not to mention the purely **financial costs** (overcharges) to farmers and consumers.

This is efficient? This is modern? Granted, for the moment, the system produces great quantities of food (at great cost), but yields are dropping.

And yet it can't provide a healthy, low-priced diet for rich-country citizens and must count on government handouts for subsidising the poorest consumers.

And it's fragile, in spite of its monolithic appearance. Imagine the collapse in case of war or an oil cutoff. My God!
So why is it tolerated?
The one word answer is Profit.
The two word answer is More Profit, for a very small minority of super-farmers and a handful of oligopolistic companies.

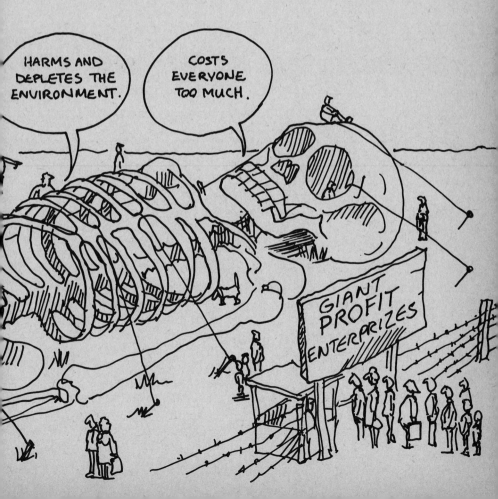

No Business Like Agribusiness

If it's not even a response to the needs of the **developed** countries, how can we imagine it would work in the Third World? It **can't** work there, and not just because it's too expensive. The whole US system was developed under unique conditions. It had lots of land, a vast frontier and relatively little labour to work it. The idea has always been to get the most out of every **person,** not out of every unit of land.

In the dominated countries, we usually find precisely the opposite conditions: relatively little land and millions of idle hands in need of productive work.

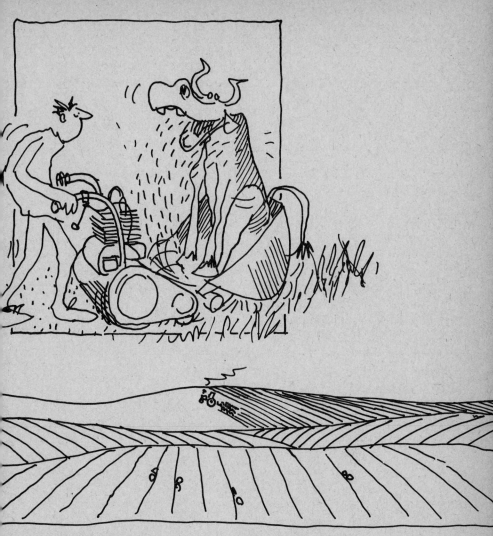

What could be dumber — if the idea is **really** to eliminate hunger — than to replace labour with capital in poor countries? At least, until other jobs are available?

Humanly dumb, maybe, but economically smart for a favoured few. Remember, corporations that dominate all sectors are not just **national** but **trans**-national. They are called **agribusinesses** and have steadily expanded operations abroad. Agribusiness is now busily re-modelling Third World food-systems along lines similar to those found in rich countries.

①

② Let's follow the food-system line for a "typical" Third World country, then see how it is changing under agribusiness pressure.

The weight of sectors **one, two, three,** is quite different where the middle segment occupies some 50 to 90% of a population. These are rural people, active, and more or less productive, in agriculture.

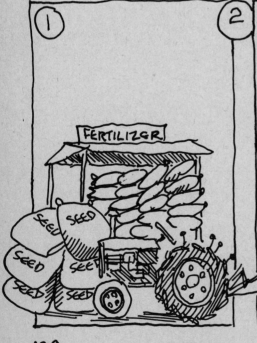

①

② Until recently, sectors one and three were not very "capital intensive". Inputs were often limited to self-reproduced seeds, animal power, simple tools and human labour (plus rain and sunshine). Where self-provisioning dominated, the producers and the consumers were the same people. They did their own storage, processing and distribution.

FERTILIZER

SEED

12-B

When food did get onto the market, it was usually a local affair. Food was sold unprocessed, or underwent simple processing like milling, in urban centres. Such things are changing fast, faster, naturally, in the better-off Third World countries where larger markets for inputs and processed foods exist; but even very poor countries are affected.

Moreover, corporations see the tropics as an inexhaustible, cheap reservoir of luxury foods. New "cash crops" — fruits, vegetables, flowers, fish and meat — have joined the traditional tea, coffee, cocoa, etc. Which means more land, labour, energy than ever devoted by poor people to feeding rich ones who already have plenty to eat.

Agribusiness makes every effort:
1. to sell its inputs or processed foods in the Third World
2. to use cheap land and labour for foods that can be sold at premium prices on Northern markets.

But agribusiness is not alone in its efforts. In fact, the groundwork is usually laid by Western government aid programmes or foundations. They provide the "infrastructure" (literally "underpinning", like roads, electric power, etc.) or the vocational education and training. Such activities are not profitable in themselves, but business can't operate without them. Agribusiness moves in when the foundations have been laid.

INPUT BILL

130

Most people in charge of Western government or foundation aid-programmes concentrate on the "technological fix" for attacking hunger. Though this approach invariably fails, it is much safer for the planners. Otherwise, they would have to confront the political and social constraints on food production and distribution. They might even have to recognise that agrarian reform and redistribution of power are necessary to eliminate hunger.

Since their bosses and the local élites they support are in no mood to entertain such notions, development planners have little choice. Technology it is. Convention also holds that anything which increases production is good. Such questions as "Production for whom?", "By whom?", are not asked.

In the 1960s, the best method, it was thought, for increasing production in underdeveloped countries was the package of techniques summed up in the slogan **Green Revolution**.

The Green Revolution

One starts with improved, "man-made" seeds that can produce high-yielding plants, usually wheat or rice. These plants respond extremely well **if** they have lots of fertiliser, chemical protection, herbicides, controlled irrigation and drainage. Since you are no longer entirely a Beginner, you have perhaps immediately asked yourself the question the planners did not: **who** would be able to use seeds that require costly, purchased inputs? The answer, of course, is the Ali/Baba kind of family — not the millions of poor cultivators with no cash reserves or access to legitimate credit.

135

The Green Revolution **does** increase production overall. Although it costs more to use, it also generally increases incomes. Even assuming that all the cultivators in a given district, regardless of size, **could** adopt GR techniques (which is not the case) at the end of the year, the richest, with the largest land-holdings will also have the largest surplus. They will use part of their profits to invest in better equipment to insure even greater productivity. They will also invest in more land. Other people's land. Northern India is one place where the GR has had some of its greatest successes and is a showcase for its defenders. Even so, a scholar basically favourable to the GR concludes that in the area, a quarter of the cultivators are "sub-marginal"; that half cannot accumulate any savings at all and thus will not improve their productivity, "nor are they in a position to withstand the vagaries of nature — drought, insect plagues or floods". We've seen what such "vagaries" can do to the most vulnerable.

As farming becomes a more and more profitable activity, landlords evict tenants and sharecroppers and farm the land themselves. They use tractors and combines to do it, too, because machines do not go on strike or make "excessive" wage demands when they notice yields improving. Fewer jobs and fewer work-days are offered. If tenants **are** allowed to stay, their rents go up. In one Indian state, "rents paid for area under (Green Revolution) varieties are more than double the rents paid under traditional crops". This is so whether or not the tenant doubles his yield. Frequently, the new seeds bring improvements of only 10-30%. Outsiders make speculative investments in land. Competition for good farming land increases enormously. In one big GR adaptor, Haryana State in India, irrigated land prices went up an average of 92% between 1966-72 in three GR villages. In a fourth village, where the

new seeds and technology didn't catch on, land prices went up only 12% during the same period. Again, only a few can afford land purchases.

Why would a rational development-planner push the Green Revolution in market economies where it was sure to increase inequalities between regions of the same country and between social classes of farmers? From the word "go" the GR was an American idea, devised by the Rockefeller and Ford Foundations.

Aid

Their research institutes developed the "miracle seeds". With the thrust of USAID behind them, they convinced governments to adopt the package. With the help of US Universities and USAID, they trained the extension workers who were to spread the word. Input salesmen, of course, followed hard on their heels. It wasn't just American trans-nationals that made the fertiliser or pesticide deals. In the case of Indonesia, for example, a lot of responsibility for pushing the package was given directly to the Swiss firm CIBA by the Indonesian government. But the companies did suddenly find a huge, new and untapped market. They were given further help by the State.

FROM 1966 THE US GOVERNMENT MADE ITS FOOD AID TO POOR COUNTRIES CONDITIONAL ON THEIR ADOPTION OF GREEN REVOLUTION TECHNIQUES. THE IDEA WAS NOT JUST TO CREATE NEW MARKETS FOR EXPANDING AMERICAN CHEMICAL OR TRACTOR INDUSTRIES, BUT ALSO TO PROMOTE "SOCIAL STABILITY." THE G.R. WAS SEEN AS AN ALTERNATIVE TO AGRARIAN REFORM, ITSELF VAGUELY EQUATED WITH "COMMUNISM."

After its heyday, it's plain that this "Revolution" increased both production **and** hunger. If this sounds paradoxical, look at India's surpluses in the late 70s. Some would argue they indicate India is now self-sufficient. Others would reply that the very existence of these stocks shows that most people are **too poor to buy them**, not that nutritional levels have risen. In fact, half of India's rural population is classed as living below a very strictly defined "poverty line". So are half the populations of the Philippines and Indonesia — other big Green Revolution customers.

So the "rational development planners" certainly haven't eliminated hunger. One must admit, however, that they got their money's worth out of the GR. Not only have they helped the sales of First World industry, but they've created strong agrarian bourgeoisies guaranteed to keep the poor and hungry "in their place", if necessary by violence. The **reported** incidents of violence of landowners against landless rural workers in India between 1974-78 amounted to over 40,000.

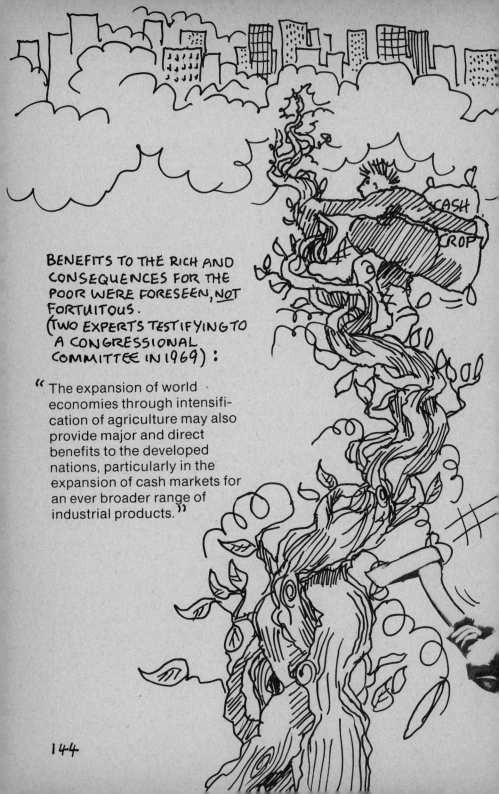

BENEFITS TO THE RICH AND CONSEQUENCES FOR THE POOR WERE FORESEEN, NOT FORTUITOUS.
(TWO EXPERTS TESTIFYING TO A CONGRESSIONAL COMMITTEE IN 1969):

" The expansion of world economies through intensification of agriculture may also provide major and direct benefits to the developed nations, particularly in the expansion of cash markets for an ever broader range of industrial products. "

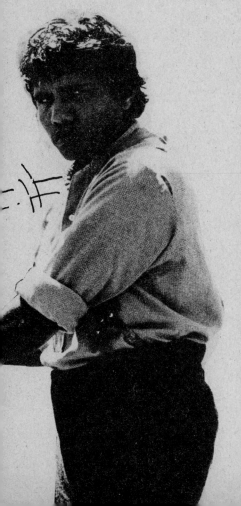

"The tenants may become a diminishing breed as they get squeezed out by landlords reclaiming their holdings because agriculture has become profitable ... Indian farmers are not going to prove any more philanthropic than any farmers anywhere ... The Green Revolution might make the rich still richer."

Agricultural workers in the industrialised countries have demanded higher wages, and production costs for foodstuffs have increased in such countries. It has thus dawned on a great many agribusiness corporations that an excellent source of supply of perishable foods is to be found in the Southern hemisphere. New-look cash crops like fruits, vegetables, flowers and meat are increasingly important in European and North American market baskets.

IN 1980, AMERICA IMPORTED $17 BILLION WORTH OF AGRICULTURAL PRODUCTS. THE USDA CLASSES THESE IMPORTS AS "COMPLEMENTARY" AND "SUPPLEMENTARY". "COMPLEMENTARY" PRODUCTS ARE TROPICAL CROPS, LIKE COFFEE OR COCOA, THAT CAN'T BE GROWN IN THE US. "SUPPLEMENTARY" IMPORTS ARE ANIMAL AND VEGETABLE PRODUCTS THAT ARE COMPETITIVE WITH AMERICA'S OWN CROPS AND LIVESTOCK. THEY PUT SUGAR IN "SUPPLEMENTARY"; BUT EVEN IF YOU ELIMINATE SUGAR, THE US IS STILL IMPORTING MORE SUPPLEMENTARY THAN COMPLEMENTARY FOOD-STUFFS.

This is a long term trend. In the 15 years from 1965-79, animal/vegetable cash crops represented 60% of all US agricultural imports, whereas for the preceding 15 years (from 1950-64) they only counted for 46%. Underdeveloped countries are supplying about a quarter of the meat and nearly three quarters of the vegetable products. Some countries with large numbers of malnourished citizens are among the biggest exporters of supplementary new-style cash crops — e.g., Mexico, Brazil, the Philippines and Thailand.

Get "back to earth"

with a truly versatile...

AMES "Rack n' Roll" cart

But among the smaller countries of Central America and the Caribbean, the proportional contributions to the affluent American diet are appalling. The Central American nations are now supplying a total of $1.5 billion in agricultural products yearly, including half a billion dollars worth of supplementaries. Caribbean island countries, particularly the Dominican Republic, now supply $250 million worth of fresh vegetable produce yearly.

The meat is usually of mediocre quality and goes straight into fast-food restaurants. Central American countries are God's gift to the burger companies and have increased their meat shipments by 70% in five years (1975-79). This can only be done by rationing the local people. Cattle for export are pastured on rich lands that could perfectly well grow food crops. Local nutritional status does a nosedive. Central Americans have had to reduce their consumption of both meat and staple cereals.

149

The fresh fruits and vegetables eliminate seasons from American tables. Fresh strawberries in February or green beans at Christmas are commonplace. Africa plays the same supplier's role for Europe. Asia supplies both North America and Japan.

HIGH YIELD GROW BOX

A consortium of corporations (something like a gaggle of geese or a pride of lions) has formed the Latin American Agribusiness Development Corporation which invests in agbiz projects (108 as of 1978). Lots of the money comes from US taxpayers via USAID. This government agency has loaned LAAD 16 million dollars at 3 or 4% interest. Try getting that from your local savings and loan! LAAD reloans (at substantially higher rates) to local businessmen or invests directly in the projects, almost all of which are devoted to export crops, not to feeding local people. As the company says, our projects "involve non-traditional exports to industrialised nations where there exists increasing demand for Latin American agricultural produce."

US Aid

THIRTY OF LAAD'S PROJECTS ARE IN GUATEMALA. HERE IS WHAT HAPPENED TO NUTRITION IN THE COUNTRY IN THE PAST FEW YEARS. PERCENT OF RURAL FAMILIES WITH INTAKES OF CALORIES AND PROTEINS BELOW THE RECOMMENDED DAILY ALLOWANCE:

ANUAL INTAKE OF MAIZE PER CAPITA 1965 204 Kgs

ANUAL INTAKE OF MAIZE PER CAPITA 1975 101·5 Kgs

PROTEINS IN 1965 27%

CALORIES IN 1965 42%

PROTEINS IN 1973 30%

CALORIES IN 1975 70%

THIS DEPLORABLE SITUATION CAN'T ALL BE BLAMED ON EXPORTS OF FOOD-STUFFS ENCOURAGED OR DIRECTLY PRACTICED BY FOREIGNERS. LAND TENURE STRUCTURES IN GUATEMALA ARE AMONG THE MOST UNJUST IN THE WORLD. BUT THE COMPANIES CERTAINLY HAVEN'T HELPED LOCAL PEOPLE. THAT'S BECAUSE LOCAL PEOPLE ARE, IN THEIR VAST MAJORITY, JUST PEOPLE. THEY'RE NOT CONSUMERS, AND CONSUMERS ARE WHAT'S WANTED.

ANOTHER CASH EXPORT FROM THE THIRD WORLD THAT HARDLY EXISTED 20 YEARS AGO IS FISH. AGAIN, THE US IS THE WORLD'S BIGGEST IMPORTER ($2 BILLION A YEAR) HERE'S HOW MONEY----THE HOOK ---CATCHES FISH IN AFRICA.

An African Fish Story

ONCE UPON A TIME, IN GHANA, THERE WAS A MACKERAL CANNERY. IT WAS SUPPLIED BY LOCAL FISHERMEN. GHANIANS ATE MACKEREL --- A CHEAP AND PLENTIFUL FISH.

BUT IN FAR-OFF AMERICA, IN 1974, AT THE HEAD-QUARTERS OF STAR-KIST TUNA (A SUBSIDIARY OF HEINZ), A CRY RESOUNDED IN THE HALLS.

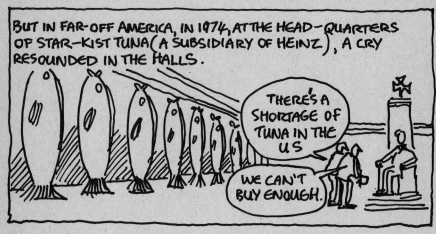

THERE'S A SHORTAGE OF TUNA IN THE US

WE CAN'T BUY ENOUGH.

STARKIST TEARFULLY WENT TO EXPLAIN ITS PROBLEM TO THE US GOVERNMENT OVERSEAS PRIVATE INVESTMENT CORPORATION (OPIC). OPIC SUPPLIES LOANS AND 'POLITICAL RISK' INSURANCE TO US TRANSNATIONAL CORPORATIONS THAT WANT TO INVEST IN THE THIRD WORLD.

SOB!

THERE THERE, DON'T CRY.

STARKIST WENT AWAY SMILING, BOUGHT ITS BOATS CAUGHT ITS FISH AND SHIPPED IT TO PUERTO RICO FOR CANNING. THEN IT WAS SOLD IN THE U.S.

BUT IN 1976, STARKIST CAME CRYING BACK TO OPIC.

NOW STARKIST COULD INVEST IN CONVERTING THE MACKEREL CANNERY TO TUNA PROCESSING. NOW THEY EXPORT TUNA FISH AND TUNA FISH CAT FOOD.

THERE ARE ABOUT 30 MILLION CATS AND 35 MILLION AMERICAN DOGS WHO ARE BETTER CUSTOMERS THAN POOR HUMAN BEINGS. IT'S 'NORMAL' THAT THIRD WORLD RESOURCES HELP TO FEED THEM.

EAT IT UP, THINK OF ALL THOSE HUNGRY PEOPLE IN THE WORLD

HOW MANY CANS CAN THIS CANNERY CAN? O P I C REPORTS 200,000 CARTONS OF TUNA FISH FOR PEOPLE AND 67,000 CARTONS OF CATFOOD (A QUARTER OF THE TOTAL PRODUCTION) FOR 1977. IT ALSO SAYS THE PLANT CAN HANDLE 20 TONS OF TUNA A DAY AND THAT GHANA SHOULD EARN $12 MILLION IN FOREIGN EXCHANGE FROM 1976 - 1981. JUST FOR FUN, LET'S WORK OUT THE BENEFITS FROM THESE FIGURES (WITH THE HELP OF BASIC DATA COLLECTED BY MY FRIEND ANN W. ON A FIELD EXPEDITION TO THE GIANT SUPERMARKET, WASHINGTON, D.C.)

AT LATE 1980 STARKIST TUNA AND NINE LIVES CATFOOD PRICES, THE COMPANY CAN SELL, OVER THE 5 YEAR PERIOD:

19,500 TONS OF TINNED PEOPLE-TUNA FOR $118,189,500
6,500 TONS OF CAT-TUNA FOR $14,462,500
    FOR A TOTAL IN SALES OF $132,652,000

ON WHICH IT CAN MAKE A MINIMUM PROFIT OF $ 5,969,300

(USING RATE OF RETURN REPORTED IN <u>FORTUNE</u>)
GHANA GETS A SMASHING 9% OF THE TOTAL VALUE OF SALES

Changing Habits

Of all the food transnationals active in the Third World, fewer than a quarter put their money into basic products needing little or no processing, like bananas, tea or vegetable oils. Those who do, make their real money at the transportation and marketing end. Fewer firms still (about 6%) make half or more of their Third World revenues by processing bulk staple foodstuffs like flour, sugar or rice. The idea is to stay out of areas where risk is highest and profit is lowest. One package of sugar or flour is much like another — there's not much reason for buying Brand X instead of Brand Y.

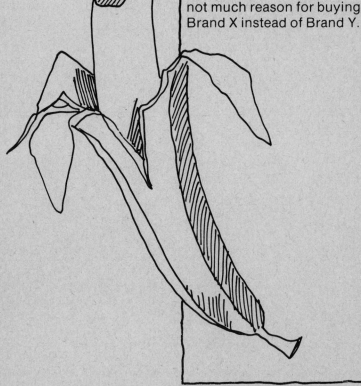

This is why some companies are moving food **out** of the poor countries, and moving their own branded products **in**. These are the same goodies manufactured in North America or Europe — the ones with maximum "value" added. The big profits are made in foods that can be "differentiated" through advertising. As the Vice-President for International Operations of Kelloggs recently put it, "The most compelling job is to change people's food habits." To change these habits — people do have these outmoded tastes for national or regional dishes — you use the same techniques that have proved successful in the rich countries. With a twist or two.

HERE ARE BUSINESS INTERNATIONAL (A TNC SUPPLYING INFORMATION AND SERVICES TO OTHER TNC'S) SALES STRATEGIES FOR THE THIRD WORLD:

SEEK TO ACHIEVE PRODUCT IDENTIFICATION AND BRAND LOYALTY THROUGH NON-VERBAL MEANS (A SYMBOLIC TRADE MARK) ESPECIALLY WHEN ILLITERACY IS WIDESPREAD .... GEAR ADS TOWARDS WOMEN SINCE THEY ARE THE PRINCIPAL CONSUMERS; PICK THE MEDIA WITH THE GREATEST PENETRATION INTO THE COUNTRYSIDE, IN RURAL AREAS WITH HIGH ILLITERACY THE RADIO IS MOST EFFECTIVE; TRY TO USE A WESTERN IMAGE TO ESTABLISH YOUR PRODUCT AS A STATUS ITEM IN DEVELOPING AREAS WHERE MODERNIZATION IS ASSOCIATED WITH WESTERNIZATION.

A VETERAN MARKETER WRITING IN A US TRADE JOURNAL IS EVEN CRUDER:
I WOULD DESCRIBE THE AVERAGE AFRICAN CONSUMER AS VERY UNSOPHISTICATED AND MORE OFTEN THAN NOT ILLITERATE. HOWEVER, HE IS VERY QUALITY CONSCIOUS AND WILLING AND ABLE TO LEARN ....(THIS MAKES HIM) VERY RECEPTIVE TO ADVERTISING.... ADVERTISE IN A MANNER WHICH WILL REACH HIM AND YOU WILL DEVELOP A CUSTOMER OF UNPRECEDENTED DEGREE OF BRAND LOYALTY AS NESTLES HAS BEEN ABLE TO DO WITH ITS CONDENSED MILK.
HERMIT AND SAGE
FIZZ
GOLDEN
INSTANT
ANDERS

The breakfast cereal companies, in particular, are committing highway robbery if you compare their cost and food value to those of traditional foods. For one Kenyan shilling, the consumer can purchase from 900 to 3630 calories if he sticks to local staples like maize or wheat flour. He only gets 40-176 calories if he buys a processed breakfast food. The large size (500 gr.) of one of these packaged cereals costs the equivalent of two days agricultural labour in the richest region of Kenya. Making people want such foods (with the "white" image) doesn't just bilk them of their cash or downgrade the cultural value of local, traditional foods. Sometimes it

can kill, as is now widely known through the "baby-foods scandal". Infant-formula companies are pushing their products to Third World mothers who have neither kitchen facilities for sterilising bottles, access to pure water nor incomes sufficient to purchase artificial milk. Mothers convinced by advertising that formula is "better" for their babies than breastmilk, mix it with impure water or overdilute the formula, or both. Infant diarrhea and death has reached such levels that the World Health Organisation has voted (with the single dissenting voice of the U S) a "code of conduct" for TNCs to control advertising and initiate a "back to breastfeeding" movement.

The TNC Invaders

Why are food TNCs invited or allowed into developing countries at all?

Brand products don't create an incentive or a market for local farmers because they are rarely based on local agricultural raw materials. Bread is a hot new item on the three poor continents, but it's almost always made of 100% imported wheat. TNC millers won't even mix local grain with the flour, so as not to have to retool their machinery.

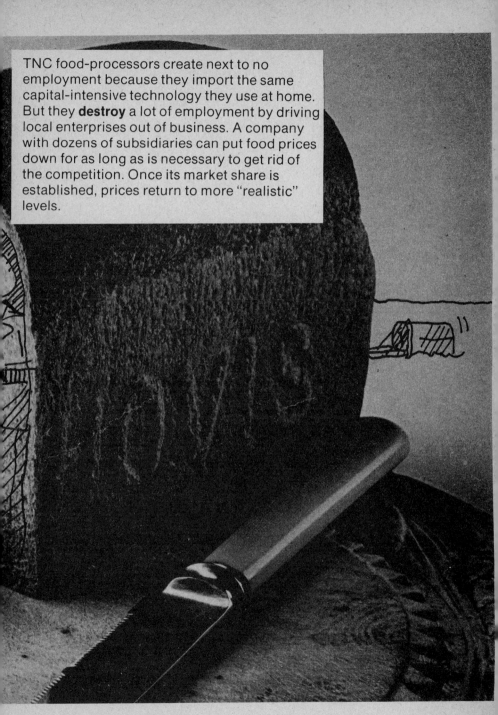

TNC food-processors create next to no employment because they import the same capital-intensive technology they use at home. But they **destroy** a lot of employment by driving local enterprises out of business. A company with dozens of subsidiaries can put food prices down for as long as is necessary to get rid of the competition. Once its market share is established, prices return to more "realistic" levels.

TNCs' junkiest brand food products are the most successful. Market expansion at four times the rate of population growth is expected for "high value-added" items like beer, candies, crackers and soft drinks. There are already at least 500 soft drink bottlers in the Third World. Coke's Chairman, speaking of the poor countries, says "The growth potential out there is unlimited." Even poor people — **especially** poor people — will pay exhorbitant sums for water, sugar and artificial flavour, and the TNCs know it. As another executive points out, "to the dismay of many would-be benefactors, the poorer the malnourished are, the more likely they are to spend a disproportionate amount of whatever they have on some luxury — like a flavoured soft drink or smoke — rather than on what they need." The malnourished market is a new target.

TNCs do not exist to help feed people, to provide employment nor to contribute to Third World development goals. No one should expect them to do so. They exist to obtain a satisfactory, not to say maximum, return on their shareholders' capital, period. The US/European food system, dominated by TNCs, can do absolutely nothing to solve the hunger problem in the Third World. It **can** provide expensive foods for those fortunate Third World consumers in a position to compete with the industrialised country affluent in the "Global Supermarket".

Third World governments that allow this food system to dominate their own, and simultaneously claim they will eliminate hunger, are either misguided or lying. Westerners, selling this system, do not eliminate hunger, but certainly help to eliminate the hungry.

What Can Be Done?

Here we near the end, and all we've done is criticise. Carp, carp, carp, and not a word on alternatives, right?

Are you upset? We hope so. If you don't feel like going out and taking a swing at someone or something, then this book is, frankly, a failure. No point is swinging blindly, though, if we've succeeded in making your adrenalin flow. Here are a few very open-ended suggestions in reply to the perennial question, "What to do?". We may as well start with what **not** to do.

Long term food aid is **not** the answer. Food aid should be saved for real emergencies (like Kampuchea). In such cases, it should be abundant, unstinting and above all, fast. Food aid-programmes should never become institutions that wear on, season after season, year after year. When this happens, aid reinforces corrupt or inept governments, discourages local food production and wipes out local farmers. In Bangladesh, the government sells food aid in special shops to card-holders — generally the urban civilian or military bureaucracies. Very little gets to hungry people in the countryside who need it. The Sahelian countries of Africa are importing 200% **more** wheat and maize than ten years ago when massive food assistance began. None of them has yet implemented a consistent grain production policy. Lots of food aid is **deliberately** geared to changing food habits (like introducing bread to Africa) and creating new commercial markets. Poor countries get hooked, then must move from "aid to trade" which means costly imports. The "food junkie" nations also become politically dependent because they can hardly bite the hand that feeds them. Most development aid (food or otherwise) from bilateral

(country to country) or multilateral (UN, World Bank) sources ends up entrenching and improving the position of the Third World dominant classes. It sounds good to finance irrigation wells to farmers, until you learn that the farmers with the most land invariably get them. Because the wells can irrigate a broader area than these farmers possess, their instinct is to get rid of tenants or buy out weaker neighbours. That's just what's happening with a big World Bank tubewell project in Bangladesh. Making the rich/poor gap even wider. Citizens of the industrialised countries who are serious about eliminating hunger should encourage a real democratic debate on aid. Taxpayers have a right to ask questions — and make their representatives ask questions — about "development" budgets. Regimes that have no intention of making their own countries more self-sufficient and egalitarian should have no claim on our money. When Marcos and Pinochet go the way of the Shah and Somoza (and it can't happen too soon), no one should be surprised if the new Filipino or Chilean leaders are wary and chary of governments whose aid did so much to maintain martial law and governments of, by, and for the TNCs.

There's nothing sacred either about the programmes of UN agencies, the World Bank or the International Monetary Fund, all of which are kept going by government contributions, i.e. us. The IMF frequently contributes to hunger by forcing poor countries to cut out all welfare measures for the most deprived. If they don't comply, they don't get loans. If they don't get loans, they go bankrupt. If we had absolute power, we would call a

moratorium on all development projects until guarantees could be given that all future projects would really benefit the worst off. Meanwhile, transfers of funds should go towards wiping out the collective debt of the Third World, now estimated at about $450 billion by those who can count that high.

We've explained why fairer and more stable prices for Third World raw materials wouldn't cure the problem, and could entrench cash crop production. Nevertheless, we should push our governments to support the Third World New Deal that goes under the catch-all name "New International Economic Order". The NIEO would at least give countries a chance to plan their land-use and expenditures more rationally. Rich countries currently blocking all progress towards this NIEO are Britain, Japan, Germany and especially the USA.

Such recommendations may sound quite dull and tame, because they involve doing some homework and lobbying. The outcome **could**, however, be important. At the very least, our governments' contributions to multilateral programmes and their behaviour in multilateral negotiations should be given a lot more scrutiny than they presently get.

If you're looking for a more exciting answer to "What to do?", the shortest and snappiest we can give you is: **Strengthen the Weak** and **Weaken the Strong**.

And don't try to do it all alone. Working with other people is important.

So is starting from where you are. You don't have to move to Calcutta or Ouagadougou to join the struggle against hunger.

Try first to understand how concentrated, minority control over your own area's food

system affects your life and the lives of people in your community. Develop an eye and a nose for the way power expresses itself close to home as one tool for better understanding oppression abroad. Even shopping can become a consciousness-raiser.

None of us is called on to take up **every** aspect of the struggle — to try is a good recipe for ineffectiveness. According to your circumstances, location, particular talents, etc., you can choose an area of concentration and a compatible group to concentrate with. You may decide the place to work is on the home front. Pressure there is vital if we are to move towards a more environment-enhancing, sustainable, people-oriented food system. Reaching that goal will involve weakening all those interests whose profits would be reduced or wiped out by change, however

beneficial that change might be for the majority. Weakening links in our present food system chain at home — like TNCs — will also weaken their influence in the dominated countries.

Try to build alliances. Food workers, small farmers and consumers have basically the same interests — and the same enemies — but they can't always see this clearly. How can we help to strengthen the weak in the dominated countries? There are plenty of groups (often called NGOs for "Non-Governmental Organisations") sponsoring development aid-projects in the Third World. Some are good and some are terrible. Stay away from the ones that worry more about "charity" than about justice. Seeking justice means first gaining a clear idea about who is oppressing whom, then encouraging the efforts of the oppressed to exercise greater

control over their own lives. **This is their job.** The role of the outsider must necessary be a supportive and secondary one. It might be limited to providing timely information or protection and embarrassing publicity if the group is threatened. A First World support group for the Third World social and political change movement must be modest. It must take its cues from those who are best able to gauge the local situation. Beware, however, of "development professionals" from poor countries. There are some, and they are experts at extracting money for spurious projects from guilt-ridden Westerners. A good rule of thumb is that the best Third World groups will aim for maximum self-reliance. They've been burned too often by foreigners — it's up to the latter to prove themselves. Remember what Bertolt Brecht said: "The enemies of the people are those who know what they need". It's up to the people themselves to define those needs.

People with real professional skills — agronomists, scientists, nutritionists, engineers and the like — who want to fight hunger can make a real contribution, if they're willing to unlearn 90% of what they've been taught and start from scratch with an open and curious mind. The Third World **does** have food production problems, but the way to solve them is **not** by copying Western methods — we hope you're convinced of that. There are no models or recipes. There are local environments, local skills and local social arrangements. On hearing this, lots of Third World people say, "You don't want us to have Western science and technology so we'll stay forever in the dark ages as your serfs." No. What's really needed is **much more**

sophisticated science and technology that has scarcely been imagined. Which is the more complex and challenging scientific problem: figuring out the right dosage of N, P, and K in a fertiliser for corn monoculture in Northeastern Iowa; or understanding the chemical and biological interactions between tree crops, bushes, standing crops and root crops of several different varieties? The obvious answer may point to why so little work has been done to raise the productivity of complex systems. It's too difficult. Scientists like problems with as few variables as possible. Research needs to be done for the poorer peasants — taking their constraints into account. Most research is consciously or unconsciously done with only the needs of the rich in mind. For instance, what's needed is plants that will give **stable** yields come drought or flood — not the **highest possible** yields under ideal conditions.

Whoever, wherever you are, keep on learning. This is a dangerous suggestion. It's dangerous for the wielders of power if your turn your sights on them, as you should definitely do. But it can be dangerous for you as well. For some people, the more they learn, the more discouraged they get. It's true that understanding reality can be depressing, because most reality **is** oppression. That's where belonging to a group can help to keep morale high. So, maybe, can these words of the Italian Marxist thinker, Gramsci, written in a Fascist prison: "Pessimism of the mind, optimism of the will".

Good luck. And loan this book to a friend.

Food Bibliography

General:
Anyone wishing seriously to pursue any aspect of the subject should work from Nicole Ball's excellent critical bibliography (over 3000 entries): *World Hunger: A guide to the economic and political dimensions;* ABC-Clio, Santa Barbara, USA and Oxford, UK 1981.

FAO publishes yearly *The State of Food and Agriculture.* Its *Monthly Bulletin of Statistics* is useful for production and trade data.

The Institute for Food and Development Policy, 1885 Mission Street, San Francisco, California 94103, has published a number of highly useful studies, among them *Food First* (Frances Moore Lappé and Joseph Collins); *Aid as Obstacle* (Lappé, Collins and David Kinley) and *Needless Hunger: Voices from a Bangladesh Village* (Betsy Hartman and James Boyce). Request the catalogue. *Food First* published in the UK by Souvenir Press, London.

The United Nations Research Institute for Social Development (UNRISD) is by far the best UN source. First rate studies on the "Green Revolution" (directed by Andrew Pearse) and on famine. Current project on "Food Systems and Society". Request the publications list from UNRISD, Palais des Nations, 1211 Geneva 10, Switzerland. Several items on the list are free of charge.

Third world trade problems, the New International Economic Order and other questions cogently and readably examined in James B. McGinnis, *Bread and Justice,* Paulist Press, New York 1979.

"Urban bias" in the Third World in Michael Lipton, *Why Poor People Stay Poor,* Temple Smith, London (and Harvard University Press) 1977.

On the "Green Revolution", in addition to the UNRISD studies (see above), Andrew Pearse, *Seeds of Plenty, Seeds of Want,* Oxford University Press 1980.

See also: Roger Burbach and Patricia Flynn, *Agribusiness in the Americas,* Monthly Review Press and NACLA, New York 1980; Pat Mooney, *Seeds of the Earth: A Public or Private Resource?,* (on the crucial question of genetic erosion, not covered in this *Beginner*) 1979, available from ICDA, Bedford Chambers, Covent Garden, London WC2.

Poverty and Landlessness in Rural Asia (various authors) International Labour Organisation, Geneva 1977.

Maketing foreign foods in Charles Medawar, *Insult or Injury?,* Social Audit, (9 Poland Street, London W1V 3DG) 1979.

Both the US Department of Agriculture and the World Bank publish food/hunger source material too voluminous to list here. You can ask for lists from USDA, Publications, Washington D.C. 20250 and the World Bank 1818 H St. NW, Washington, D.C. 20433 or 66, Avenue d'Iéna, 75116 Paris, France.

Some sources used for this book:

On hunter-gatherers and the origins of agriculture: Marshall Sahlins, *Stone Age Economics,* Tavistock, London 1974; J.V.S. Megaw (ed.) *Hunters, Gatherers and First Farmers beyond Europe* (see especially the contribution by Warwick Bray); Leicester University Press in the UK; Humanities Press, New Jersey in the US. Full of leads to further reading for those interested. Grahame Clark and Stuart Piggott; *Prehistoric Societies,* Penguin, Harmondsworth, 1970.

On peasants and various historical matters: The definition of a peasant is Teodor Shanin's. See Shanin (ed.) *Peasants and Peasant Societies,* Penguin, Harmondsworth, 1971; Andrew Pearse, *The Latin American Peasant,* Frank Cass, London 1976; Georges Duby, *L'Economie Rurale et la Vie des Campagnes dans l'Occident Médiéval,* Flammarion, Paris 1977 and Fernand Braudel's massive three volume study (shortly to appear in English) *Civilisation Matérielle, Economie et Capitalisme XVe – XVIIIe Siècles,* Armand Colin, Paris 1979.

The best comprehensive book on the Irish famine is Cecil Woodham-Smith, *The Great Hunger,* New English Library, London 1965.

On colonialism: Walter Rodney, *How Europe Underdeveloped Africa,* Bogle-l'Ouverture, London 1972; Robert Rhodes (ed.) *Imperialism and Underdevelopment,* Monthly Review Press, New York 1970. Examining colonialism but also present day hunger problems of the Sahelian countries is Richard Franke and Barbara Chasin's excellent *Seeds of Famine,* Allanheld, Osmun & Co., Montclair, N.J. 1980.

Pierre Spitz gave me his usual generous help and useful criticism. In particular, the model of the effects of drought on various families, is his and his alone. I am simply trying to give it a wider audience than it will find in "Drought and Self-Provisioning", UNRISD Working Paper, 1980 (available from UNRISD as above) or as published in J. Ausubel and A. Biswas (eds.) *Climatic Constraints and Human Activities,* Pergamon Press, Oxford. Some of Pierre's other articles include: "The Public Granary", *Ceres-FAO Magazine,* November-December 1979, "Silent Violence: Famine and Inequality", *International Social Sciences Journal,* Vol. XXX, no. 4, 1978; also in *Violence and its Causes, UNESCO, 1980;* "Livelihood and the Food Squeeze", *Ceres-FAO* Magazine, May-June 1981.

Dan Morgan, *Merchants of Grain,* Viking, New York 1979; thoroughly and entertainingly describes the doings of the giant companies who control world food trade.

The New Internationalist is a lively monthly with excellent articles on problems of underdevelopment, including hunger. Subscriptions, UK: Clair Beckwith, the *NI,* Montagu House, High St., Huntingdon PE18 6EP, Cambs.; USA & Canada: the *NI,* 113 Atlantic Avenue, Brooklyn, N.Y. 11201.

Readers interested in my other work on food and hunger may consult Susan George, *How the Other Half Dies: The real reasons* for world hunger, Penguins in the UK; Allanheld, Osmun & Co. Montclair, N.J. in the USA; *Feeding the Few: Corporate Control of Food* is available (as is the US edition of 'The Other Half') from the publisher: Institute for Policy Studies, 1901 Que Street NW, Washington, D.C. 20009 ($3.95).

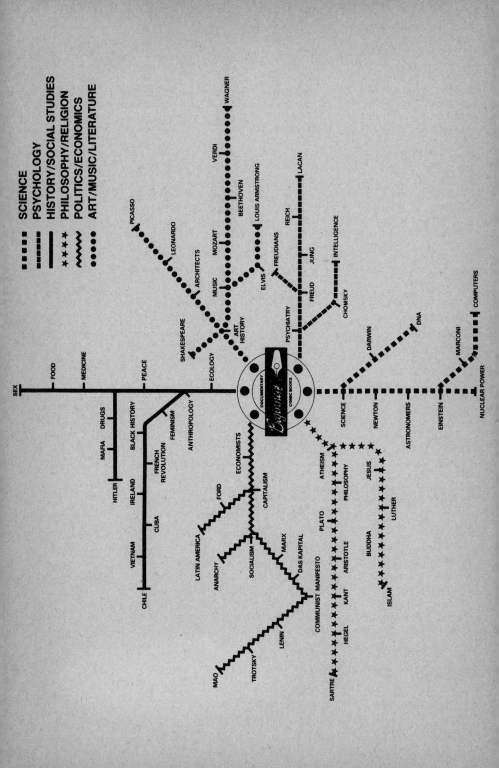